D1270000

Contemporary
Military
Strategy

Written under the auspices of
The Center for International Affairs
Harvard University

Contemporary Military Strategy

MORTON H. HALPERIN

Harvard University

LITTLE, BROWN AND COMPANY

Boston

Acknowledgment

My great debt is to my fellow military strategists whose ideas I have attempted to summarize in this volume. The most important items on which I have drawn are identified in the selected reading at the end of each chapter; I have also benefited from numerous papers and conversations.

Many of the chapters in this book were first delivered in a much earlier form as lectures in a course on contemporary military strategy given in the fall of 1963 at the University of London and in the spring of the same year at the Graduate Institute of International Studies in Geneva. I am grateful to Professors Michael Howard, and Louis Halle and Jacques Freymond for the invitations which brought me to their respective Institutes and to the Rockefeller Foundation for financial support during part of that period.

Chapter Six on Chinese military strategy is based in part on a paper in Alastair Buchan, ed., *China and the Peace of Asia* (New York: Praeger, for the Institute for Strategic Studies, 1965). Chapter Eleven on deterrence and defense of Asia is a revised version of a paper originally prepared for the Sandia Corporation. I am grateful to the Institute for Strategic Studies and to the Sandia Corporation for permission to use this material. I have discussed issues of limited war in more detail in my book *Limited War in the Nuclear Age* (New York: Wiley, 1963).

It is a pleasure to record my debt to the Center for International Affairs for continuing to support my research and for providing a setting uniquely appropriate for the writing of this volume.

My wife has not kept pace but she has prepared the index and worked her magic on the text.

Cambridge, Mass.   Morton H. Halperin
May, 1966

Table of Contents

ix

Contemporary
Military
Strategy

CHAPTER ONE

The Role of Force
in the Nuclear Age

This book examines from the perspective of the major powers the role of force in international politics in the age of the nuclear missile. It is based on the assumption, which will be examined briefly in this chapter, that force does continue to play a role despite the development of thermonuclear weapons and intercontinental ballistic missiles. The approach taken here to the role of force in the Nuclear Age may be contrasted with several absolute views about the nature of war in the current period. Holders of the first of these views argue that nuclear weapons have abolished war: that war has become unthinkable and impossible. Their line of thinking is that because nuclear weapons now exist, all war would be total war; therefore, war will not take place. The events of the postwar period, however, make it clear that the invention of atomic weapons has not made war impossible. In fact, while major world war has been avoided, the amount of violence in the world—however it is measured—has not been appreciably reduced. Nuclear weapons, then, have not abolished war; war very much remains a thinkable and possible instrument of policy.

A second view suggests that while nuclear weapons have not yet made war impossible, war must be abolished if mankind is to survive. Those who adhere to this theory argue that unless all war is abolished, we will eventually have a nuclear war that will destroy most, if not all, of civilization. But this approach does not suggest how one can go about abolishing war. Nor does it demonstrate that nuclear war is inevitable unless all violence is eliminated.

Supporters of a third, somewhat less extreme, approach contend that while war may continue, *nuclear* war has now become "unthinkable": either a nuclear war will never occur or nuclear war must be prevented if mankind is to survive. Some who hold this opinion would argue that nuclear war should not be studied, for to study nuclear war is to allow that such a war is thinkable and acceptable, and therefore more likely. A counter view—the view maintained throughout this book—holds that since nuclear war may occur, despite our best efforts to avoid it, it is necessary to try to understand what a nuclear war might be like. In any case, the threat of nuclear war and of the use of nuclear weapons plays a significant role in international politics. Even if, as appears likely, there never is a nuclear war, the invention of nuclear weapons will have had a profound effect on the course of international politics and, indeed, on the course of human history.

A fourth, more extreme approach advocates preventive nuclear war to produce peace. This approach suggests that a nuclear war is in the long run inevitable; therefore, the sooner the better. Implicit in this theory, then, is the belief that human violence can be ended but that preventive war, not international disarmament, is the means to this utopia.

Each of the approaches discussed above prescribes how nations should act, and each proposes substantial changes. This book will adopt a more descriptive technique by examining the changes in the behavior of nations in the Nuclear Age. In addition, marginal changes, which might improve the military situation, will be suggested.

Does force, both in its employment and the threat of its employment, affect the behavior of nations and of individuals? The answer seems clearly to be yes, despite the development of nuclear weapons. Therefore, one must consider how, in fact, force does affect behavior in the current period, in contrast to the pre-Nuclear Age.

Through the ages, the evolution of technology for warfare has been marked by a search for, as well as a fear of, the absolute weapon. At various times men have thought the crossbow, the machine gun, and the airplane the absolute weapon, which, depending upon one's point of view, would either enable one state to dominate the world or would force all men to live in peace. The destruction of Hiroshima and Nagasaki led some people to describe the atomic bomb as "the absolute weapon." It has since become clear that the atomic bomb alone is not the ultimate weapon, and the search has gone on for this weapon in the form of intercontinental missiles, submarine-launched missiles, and others. While recognizing that we are never likely to obtain anything that can really be called an absolute weapon, it is important to have some understanding of the changes in weapon technology that have occurred with the development of the atomic, and then the hydrogen, bomb; namely, the destructive power of weapons and the ability to deliver them.

The destructive power of weapons should be thought of in terms of its yield to weight ratio; that is, how much destruction is caused for each given pound of explosive material. The base taken for comparison in describing the destructive power of nuclear weapons is the weight of a TNT bomb that would cause the same destruction. The yield of an atomic bomb is expressed in the equivalent of one thousand pounds of TNT (kilotons) or one million pounds of TNT (megatons); that is, a two-megaton bomb has the equivalent destructive power of two million tons of TNT.

The destructive power of weapons has increased enormously twice during the Atomic Age. The first atomic weapons, the so-called fission bombs, had a destructive power a thousand times greater per pound than traditional TNT or other high explosive weapons. The hydrogen, or fusion, bomb was again a thousand times more powerful per pound than fission weapons. Thus, the two revolutions in fire power have produced a millionfold increase in power for a given weight.

Another way to indicate this changed magnitude of destruction is to say that one American bomber now carries more than the total destructive power of all the weapons dropped in all the wars in human history. The largest bombs of World War II were the equivalent of approximately *five* tons of TNT, and the Hiroshima bomb was equal to approximately *twenty thousand* tons of TNT. Current American nuclear weapons have yields from tenths of a kiloton to *one million* tons on the warhead of the Minuteman intercontinental missile and *twenty million* tons in America's large intercontinental bombers.

The fantastic increase in the destructive power of weapons has almost been matched by improvements in the ability to deliver these weapons. ICBM's possessed by the Soviet Union and by the United States can reach any point on the globe from any other point within thirty to forty minutes with incredible accuracy. This accuracy is expressed in terms of a *CEP* (circular error probability). The number identified as the CEP is the radius of a circle within which half of all the fired weapons land. For example, if four missiles with a CEP of two miles were fired at a target, two of the missiles would land within two miles of the target. In these terms, American and Soviet missiles appear to have a CEP of considerably less than two miles. Superpowers thus can fire missiles five thousand miles or more and have half of their missiles land within two miles of their target.

The development and deployment of ballistic-missile defenses (BMD) by the United States and the Soviet Union would affect the number of missiles that can reach their target but would not alter the basic facts: both of the superpowers have thermonuclear weapons a million times more powerful than World War II weapons and both can deliver these weapons with intercontinental missiles in about thirty minutes. In trying to understand the impact of thermonuclear weapons on international politics, it is important to keep in mind these two very general quantitative developments.

In the postwar period these changes in technology have been accompanied by an essential bipolarity of power centered around the United States and the Soviet Union. Some countries, most recently France and China, have challenged the policies of the superpowers. However, the two leading countries still dominate, at least in part because they are the only powers possessing substantial nuclear capability. The postwar period has also been marked by intense ideological conflict between colonial and excolonial powers and between the Communist and non-Communist world.

THE MILITARY BALANCE

While analysts have argued about whether or not military force still has a role to play, governments have been under no illusion about the consequences of not having adequate military capability. Both the United States and the Soviet Union have spent very large sums of money, perhaps exceeding the combined total of one hundred billion dollars for the development of nuclear forces and their delivery systems. To assess the role of nuclear weapons, it is important to have some understanding of the nuclear and conventional forces existing on both sides. These will be considered in terms of strategic nuclear forces, tactical nuclear forces, and conventional forces.

Strategic Nuclear Forces

Through the 1960's the American strategic nuclear force will consist of a very large missile force and a moderate number of intercontinental bombers in addition to shorter-range, fighter-bomber aircraft and missiles in Europe and perhaps elsewhere. When the present program is completed, the missile force will consist of 1,000 Minuteman intercontinental ballistic missiles—kept in well-protected underground silos in the United States and capable of reaching all of the Soviet Union—and 656 Polaris missiles. The yield of these weapons is approximately one megaton. The United States also has some older Titan II missiles that can carry a much larger warhead, perhaps as high as eight to ten megatons, but that burn a liquid fuel and consequently can neither be fired as quickly or as efficiently as the Minuteman or Polaris nor can they be as well protected.

There has been much controversy about the role that manned bombers can play in a period in which intercontinental missiles have dominated the strategic scene. While the importance of bombers has declined, it seems clear that both the United States and the Soviet Union will maintain some bomber fleets through the rest of the decade and into the 1970's. The American bomber force, some of which is on airborne alert and much of which is on ground alert, has been declining in size in the 1960's; but a fleet of at least two hundred bombers will be kept in service into the

1970's. Bombers can carry either several bombs of twenty mega-tons or more, or a number of smaller bombs, perhaps fired from air-to-surface missiles.

The major addition to the American capability for attacking targets in the Soviet Union will be the F-111. While designed primarily to attack military targets on the battlefield, the F-111, particularly in a special bomber version, will be able to carry a significant nuclear payload—that is, a number of bombs—over desired targets. The United States will be producing more than one thousand of these bombers, and as many as two hundred might be modified for the strategic bombing role.

The Soviet strategic nuclear force (discussed in Chapter Five) appears to be much smaller and much less sophisticated than the American force. From all reports, the Soviets have less than half the number of intercontinental missiles the United States has. These missiles burn liquid fuel and react more slowly than the American Minuteman but carry a much larger payload. The Soviets also have a small bomber force that can reach the United States. The bulk of the Soviet strategic nuclear capability is concentrated in approximately one thousand medium-range and intermediate-range missiles (MRBM's and IRBM's)—that is, missiles that go a distance of fifteen hundred miles or less—stationed in the western part of the Soviet Union and targeted on Western Europe, with the capability of destroying any desired targets in Western Europe.

Tactical Nuclear Forces

Since the mid-1950's the United States has built up an impressive array of so-called tactical nuclear weapons; that is, nuclear weapons designed to support land forces, particularly in Europe. Developments in this area have given the United States a capability in the form of nuclear weapons from extremely low yields—below that of the largest conventional weapons—to a kiloton, and larger weapons for attacking air bases and other large targets. American stockpiles of tactical nuclear weapons in Europe have grown steadily during the first half of the 1960's to a force of weapons numbering in the thousands; these weapons are carried by a variety of delivery systems. The Soviets are reported to have a much smaller and less varied arsenal of tactical nuclear weapons consisting mainly of short-range rockets with warheads in the kiloton range.

Conventional Forces

It is important to recognize that despite the growth of nuclear power and the increasing sophistication of the arsenals of the two superpowers, both the United States and the Soviet Union, as well as their allies, have maintained large conventional ground forces. While it is true that these forces might be employed along with tactical nuclear weapons, they also have the capability to fight alone. The United States and its NATO allies have put less emphasis than the Soviet Union and China have on spending for conventional ground forces, although the United States substantially increased its spending for these forces in the 1960's. Whatever the relative emphasis, it is important to realize that all of the major powers spend more than half of their military budgets on conventional forces, much of it on salaries. Thus, along with their nuclear capabilities, the superpowers have a very real ability to fight conventionally.

THE ROLE OF MILITARY FORCE

We can consider the role of existing military power in terms of its effect on peacetime diplomacy, crises, conventional wars, and nuclear conflict.

Peacetime Diplomacy

The great expense involved in developing large, sophisticated thermonuclear capabilities has been one of the prime reasons for the maintenance of bipolarity. Only the United States and the Soviet Union have been able to afford such weapons. The United States, for example, spends on defense approximately three times the total United Kingdom budget and six times the British defense budget. Similar, perhaps greater, disparities exist between the Chinese and the American and Russian budgets. Thus, while France, Britain, and China have begun to develop nuclear capabilities, the Soviet Union and the United States are—and are likely to remain for quite awhile—the two giant and dominant super-powers.

The existence of thermonuclear weapons has forced the two superpowers to take a new view of their relations. Under a classic balance of power we would expect the two main powers to be in total conflict with each other and to seek support from various other countries in an effort to tip the balance. However, particularly in the last several years, the two superpowers have come to see that while there are many things that separate them, they are joined by a common desire to avoid thermonuclear war. This insight has led to pressure for *détente* in both the United States and the Soviet Union. The search for disarmament and arms-control agreements has changed in focus and emphasis from the attempt of idealists to create a world of total peace to an attempt by realists to improve the nature of the military balance and to reduce the likelihood of general nuclear war. Thus, in a world situation in which conflict between the superpowers remains great, we have had the partial test ban treaty and other measures, including the "hot line" agreement linking the United States and the Soviet Union with a high-speed, reliable communication system. The greater emphasis on agreement between the two super-powers, particularly in the arms-control area, must be attributed almost entirely to their destructive potentialities. As former Soviet Premier Nikita Khrushchev put it, "The atom bomb recognizes no class differences."

The fear of thermonuclear war has led the superpowers to try to avoid situations of intense international political crisis. Both sides have refrained from pressing political advantages that might upset the military balance. There has also been extreme caution in the use of conventional military forces. Thus, the Soviet Union has never actually employed its conventional capabilities to seize Berlin; and the United States has, in the end, refrained from an effective invasion of Cuba. While other restraints have been operative in both cases, the fear of setting in motion a chain of events that might lead to general nuclear war has been a dominant factor.

The same pressures have compelled the superpowers to become more directly involved in local conflicts throughout the world. The Soviet Union and the United States believe that any conflict runs the risk of precipitating general nuclear war. There has been a tendency, particularly on the part of the United States, to intervene quickly at the first sign of local conflict in order to isolate the conflict and to halt the fighting before it spreads to general war.

Crises

Caution has marked the approach of the superpowers to crises as well as to peacetime diplomacy. Both sides have sought to contain quickly any spontaneous crisis, such as the Hungarian uprising of 1956. Even in crises induced by one of the two superpowers—for example, the Cuban missile crisis in 1962—both sides have acted in a cautious way designed to reduce the likelihood of general war and to end the conflict as quickly as possible. This is not to say that the superpowers and their allies have not sought to get political advantage from a crisis. It is simply to note that their willingness to maneuver and to seek advantage has been severely limited by the nature of the overall military balance. In fact, the history of postwar crises suggests that the probability of nuclear war has—if anything—been exaggerated and has tended to dominate the thinking of decision-makers during a crisis. One has only to recall Mr. Khrushchev's statements about the world being close to thermonuclear war during the Cuban missile crisis or to read memoirs of American leaders at that time to realize the extent to which top leaders will allow this problem to influence their views. Because of the fear of a general nuclear war and the desire to end the conflict quickly, local conventional military power, which could be brought to bear quickly, has tended to be critical in crises such as those in Hungary and in Cuba.

Conventional War

The existence of thermonuclear weapons has made extremely unlikely another very large-scale military conflict of the order of World War I or World War II. While neither of the superpowers has ruled out such a conflict in developing its military capabilities, neither seems to attach high priority to the probability of such a war. Nor if such a war were to occur, would it likely remain conventional and limited. Further, with the improbability of world-wide, general war, has come an increase in local conventional wars—both international and, more frequently, civil—for example, in Vietnam, Laos, Greece, and Korea. Such wars have all been fought under the shadow of the nuclear deterrent capability of the two superpowers; that is, the actions of the superpowers in these conflicts have been influenced by their belief that local conflicts could explode into general nuclear war. Though this phenomenon has led to the exercise of restraint on the part of the superpowers in the exploitation of success in local conflict, it has nevertheless been the case that local conventional military forces and local political factors have tended to dominate and determine the outcome of any particular military clash. Limited local wars, including guerrilla wars, have been an instrument of international political change and have become, to a large extent, the ultimate arbitrator of political conflict because nobody wants to use the real, ultimate weapons—the nuclear weapons.

Nuclear War

The United States and the Soviet Union have been willing to allow conventional and local political factors to determine the outcome of much conflict in the postwar period precisely because this conflict does not threaten the vital interests of the superpowers. However, it is clear that nuclear weapons would remain the final arbiter when and if the vital interests of the superpowers were challenged. This produces what many observers have pointed to as the central paradox of the Nuclear Age: total ideological conflict plus total means of destruction have produced a situation in which a total solution is impossible. The major powers compete with each other in non-military ways and in the use of conventional military force but with no hope of total military victory. Whatever we may choose to call it, we are doomed to peaceful coexistence with our enemies because we live in a world in which war cannot be abolished, because there is no other means to settle issues that men feel are worth fighting for. But war—at least war in the sense of general nuclear war—can only lead to such complete destruction that in the final analysis, the war could not have been worth fighting. It is this central paradox which provides the challenge and the setting for discussion of the role of military strategy in the current era.

SELECTED BIBLIOGRAPHY

Herz, John H. *International Politics in the Atomic Age.* New York: Columbia University Press, 1959.

Kissinger, Henry A. *Nuclear Weapons and Foreign Policy.* New York: Harper, 1957.

Schelling, Thomas C. *Arms and Influence.* New Haven: Yale University Press, 1966.

Tucker, Robert W. *The Just War.* Baltimore: Johns Hopkins Press, 1960.

Waltz, Kenneth N. *Man, the State, and War.* New York: Columbia University Press, 1959.

CHAPTER TWO

Warfare in the Nuclear Age

The changes in the nature of military technology outlined briefly in Chapter One and the subsequent impact of these changes on international politics have aroused much attention, particularly on the part of students of international politics. This interest has produced new terminology and new concepts that help explain the nature of military power in the Nuclear Age.

The most pervasive notion is that of "deterrence": that the primary function of military force should be to prevent the use of military force by one's opponents. The great destructive power of nuclear weapons has forced students of international politics to take more seriously the possibility of eliminating or substantially reducing the likelihood of war and, in particular, of large-scale thermonuclear war. The recognition that conflict is likely to remain a part of the international political scene, coupled with the belief that thermonuclear war would be so devastating as to be unacceptable, has led to the development of a typology of warfare and to an emphasis on the possibilities and problems of limiting war.

The first attempt to divide wars into categories came with the distinction made between "limited" wars and "total" wars. A limited war was viewed as a conflict that would not involve the homelands of the United States or the Soviet Union and that would remain limited both in objectives and in the means used. A total war, on the other hand, was a war involving attacks on the homelands of the United States and the Soviet Union. It was assumed that in such a war there would be no limit on either the objectives or the means employed.

More recently analysts have felt the need to use the terms "general" and "local" to distinguish wars. A *general war*, as the term will be used in this book, is defined as a war involving attacks by the United States and the Soviet Union on each other's homelands. A *local war* is defined as a war in which the United States and the Soviet Union (or China) see themselves on opposite sides but in which no attacks are made on the homelands of the two superpowers. As will be indicated below, both a local war and a general war could be a "limited" war—as the term has been used —limited in objectives or in the means used and targets attacked.

GENERAL WAR

Beginning about 1964 the world finally entered the missile age that had been heralded at least since 1957. By the middle of the 1960's the major strategic nuclear forces (or in the Pentagon's terms, the strategic offensive forces) of the United States and the Soviet Union were ballistic missiles. Missiles became part of the arsenals of both countries in the late 1950's, but until the mid-sixties the airplane remained the dominant mode for delivery of nuclear weapons. Missiles with their smaller payload and their potentialities for greater control over operations have made more realistic the possibility and desirability of controlling a general nuclear war, should one occur. In attempting to analyze the possibilities for limitation in general nuclear war, three kinds of wars involving the use of strategic attacks on the homelands of the United States and the Soviet Union have been identified.

Spasm War

At least throughout the 1950's American statements and planning seemed to be based upon the assumption that a general nuclear war between the United States and the Soviet Union would be an all-out, or "spasm," war. It was believed that a general nuclear war could not be limited. Therefore, it was envisioned that if a general nuclear war was started, each side would fire all of its nuclear weapons at the other side as quickly as possible in a spasm reaction to the beginning of war. In such a war each side would presumably fire all its strategic forces at military and population targets in the other's homeland. As will be indicated more fully in Chapter Four, the Soviet Union continues to talk publicly about general nuclear war in spasm-war terms.

Controlled Response

If one recognizes that the all-out, uncontrolled use of nuclear weapons by both superpowers would lead to very substantial destruction of the population and industry of the two countries, then it becomes clear that both sides might attempt to limit a general nuclear war, should one take place. Even a large-scale nuclear war might be limited in terms of the targets attacked: each side might refrain from bombing the other's major cities and might concentrate instead on military targets. In addition, each side might not use all of its strategic forces, holding some in reserve with which to threaten the destruction of its opponent's cities.

Limited Strategic Strikes

At the opposite extreme from spasm war is the proposal that strategic nuclear weapons might be used in very limited numbers. The possibilities in this category range from the very bizarre notion of one side's destroying one or several of its opponent's cities to the perhaps somewhat more likely possibility of engaging in very limited strategic strikes at military or industrial targets far from the centers of population. Such strikes might be used either to influence the course of a local war that is in progress or to demonstrate a willingness to go to large-scale general nuclear war if necessary.

Motivations for War Initiation

A general nuclear war may be a *deliberate war*; that is, a war consciously and deliberately initiated by one of the two superpowers while that superpower is fully cognizant of its option to avoid such a war. Without being able to rule out entirely the possibility of a deliberate nuclear war, most analysts contend that *inadvertent war* is much more likely, given the relative destruction that would occur to both countries. An inadvertent war is one that occurs because one or both sides come to the conclusion that whatever the intentions of the two superpowers, general nuclear war has for some reason become inevitable. In this situation, the leadership beginning the war does so believing that the choice is not between general nuclear war or no general nuclear war but rather between general nuclear war which it has initiated or which has been initiated by its adversary. In this situation the motive for war is simply the belief that war will occur and that it is better to strike first or at least be a close, rather than a distant, second.

Triggers of Nuclear War

The very destructive power of nuclear weapons and the inability of the bureaucracy in the United States or the Soviet Union to guarantee to the top leadership that destruction would be kept to tolerable levels, even with a first strike, has minimized the probability of a deliberately initiated general nuclear war. However, there are certain situations in which one side or the other might be tempted to launch a deliberate strike.

If one of the superpowers believed it could escape substantial retaliation because of a lack of diligence on the part of its opponent in developing strategic systems capable of surviving an attack and penetrating active defenses, it might be tempted to launch such a strike. However, even if calculations suggested that there would not be substantial retaliation, political leaders might find it difficult to believe the calculations. And even if they believed them, they would not necessarily decide to begin war. In the late 1940's the United States had a monopoly that would have enabled it to strike the Soviet Union with nuclear weapons without fearing retaliation. While it is possible that, in the same position, the Soviet Union would not pass up such an opportunity, it is perhaps more likely that it would exploit the situation for political purposes rather than actually carry out a deliberate nuclear strike. Nevertheless, while analysts can assert that the probability of a deliberate nuclear strike is extremely low, governments on both sides have felt obliged to spend a great deal of money and devote a good deal of time to making sure that their opponent will never come to the conclusion that a successful first strike is possible.

A deliberate strike might also be carried out if the leadership in one country believed that the consequences of not starting a nuclear war were even more devastating than the outcome of a nuclear war. For example, the Soviet leaders *might* resort to all-out nuclear war if Communist control of Eastern Europe appeared to be threatened, and if they believed that there was no other way of preventing the establishment of regimes friendly to the West. During the Cuban missile crisis of 1962, the United States threatened to initiate a general war if the Soviet Union or Cuba fired a single missile from Cuban territory that landed anywhere in the Western Hemisphere.

Finally, at least in principle, one cannot rule out complete irrationality; that is, a decision to launch general nuclear war for reasons unrelated to the direct consequences of the outcome of the war, perhaps involving personal, psychological impulses. The governments of both the United States and the Soviet Union have taken steps to insure that irrational action below the very top level of government could not lead to a general war. Though it is difficult to evaluate the effectiveness of these steps, they appear to be extremely reliable and to reduce to the barest minimum the possibility of a war triggered by the irrationality of a subordinate. Irrationality of the top leadership is, of course, more difficult to prevent by formal institutional means; and it should not be forgotten that Stalin demonstrated some tendencies of a mentally unbalanced person, although probably not those which might have led him to launch a general nuclear war.

Much more likely than the triggering of a deliberate nuclear war is the triggering of an inadvertent general nuclear war. However, the two dangers interact with each other: the higher the probability of a deliberate attack, the greater the danger of an inadvertent general nuclear war. In order for an inadvertent war to take place, there must be first, a belief in the high probability of war, and second, a perceived value of striking first if war occurs. A reduction in either of these would substantially reduce the possibility of a general nuclear war.

The perception that general nuclear war is impending depends on, in turn, both a conducive setting and some triggering event. Neither the leadership of the United States nor that of the Soviet Union is likely to conclude in a period of international calm that the probability of general nuclear war is so high that it is necessary to strike first. Only during an intense political crisis, such as has occurred from time to time over Berlin and over Cuba, or in a setting of local war, such as occurred in Korea or Indochina, might the superpowers be inclined to feel that a general nuclear war is imminent. The triggering event that then precipitates the general nuclear war may be one of several incidents. It may be a literal accident; that is, the detonation of a nuclear weapon or the firing of a missile because of mechanical or human failure. Another possibility—although remote—is an attempt by a country other than the United States or the Soviet Union to simulate the beginning of a nuclear war, perhaps again by exploding a nuclear device. Finally, the trigger may simply come from the expansion of the local war or crisis: the war may become so intense that one side resorts to general nuclear war.

Even if the probability of general nuclear war seems high, the occurrence of an inadvertent war depends on the perception of a great value in striking first should war occur. During the early 1960's the world passed through a period in which both sides appeared to believe that in the event of nuclear war, there was a very high value in striking first. This was partly because neither side had paid sufficient attention to developing forces able to survive a first strike but also because, in the period of transition from airplanes to missiles, a very small number of missiles seemed capable of destroying a very large number of airplanes in a surprise first strike.

Within the last several years the United States and, to a lesser degree, the Soviet Union have paid greater attention to the *vulnerability* of strategic forces to a surprise first strike. Both sides have developed relatively invulnerable forces; that is, forces difficult to destroy in a first strike and designed to ride out the first strike of the opponent. This relative invulnerability is developed in three ways: concealment, hardening, and mobility. The Russians have relied for several years on concealment of the location of their strategic forces; however, improvements in intelligence capacities, particularly cameras in satellites, have rendered this method of developing relative invulnerability comparatively ineffective. Hardening is used for the American Minuteman missiles, which are in hardened underground sites in the western part of the United States; and mobility gives relative invulnerability to the American Polaris missile-firing submarines, which keep in constant motion under the vast oceans. As strategic forces have become relatively invulnerable, the Unitel States at least has come to the conclusion that if it is confronted with a Soviet first strike, it should not launch its weapons until after a significant number of Soviet missiles have landed on American territory. The United States has tried to make it clear to the Soviet Union that it has adopted this position, which should substantially reduce the probability of an inadvertent general nuclear war launched by either power. By removing fear of an American inadvertent strike, the Soviet need to strike first should be diminished.

LOCAL WAR

As has been indicated earlier, analysts have attempted to distinguish general strategic nuclear war from local war. A local nuclear war is by definition limited in that it excludes the homelands of the two superpowers. However, there have been a number of other limits observed in local wars that have taken place in the postwar period. In this connection, it is important to remember that while analyses of general nuclear war must fortunately proceed simply on the basis of theoretical analysis, discussion of local non-nuclear war can draw on relevant historical examples as well.

If we look at the history of local war since World War II, we discover four kinds of limitations that have apparently been of great importance in keeping a local war from becoming a general nuclear war. The first of these involves the geography of the area in which the fighting is taking place. Not only have the homelands of the two superpowers been spared in all warfare, but so has much of the rest of the world. Each of the local wars that has taken place has been confined to a relatively small geographic area: the Taiwan Straits, Korea, Indochina, Cuba and its surrounding waters, and others.

Perhaps the most important limit that has been observed in local war in the postwar period has been the reluctance to use nuclear weapons. Neither of the two superpowers, when engaged in military action, has employed those weapons that, even at the tactical level, are judged to be most effective.

Another limitation that has been observed in many local wars but violated or ignored by the United States in Cuba and more recently in Vietnam is the sanctity of supply lines beyond the area of battle. What was spectacular about American action in Cuba was that the United States sought for the first time since the Second World War to interfere with the movement of materiel into the area of potential conflict. Later in Vietnam the United States again ignored the "sanctuary" of North Vietnam and began to destroy supply lines moving into the area of battle. However, there remain even in the Vietnamese war important target limitations. For example, the United States, at least until the end of 1965, refrained from attacking the major cities of North Vietnam.

The fourth major category of limitation concerns the level of participation of various countries in the local war. The two superpowers and China have been concerned with avoiding a direct confrontation of the troops of two of these countries. There has, of course, not been any direct confrontation of Soviet and American formal military forces; even in Korea where American and Chinese troops clashed, American troops were disguised as part of a UN command and Chinese troops as volunteers. American actions in Vietnam in the 1960's demonstrate clearly the spectrum of roles that a superpower can play in relation to a local war. The United States began the decade providing diplomatic and economic support for the government of South Vietnam. It moved from that to providing military equipment and limited amounts of training on the ground in South Vietnam through a series of other steps leading up to the use of American combat troops in the war against the Vietcong.

How important the territory being fought over is to the superpowers is another key factor in determining the outcome and consequences of a local war. Some territories are more important to one of the superpowers than to another. For example, the United States recognized the greater Soviet interest in Hungary and greater Chinese interest in Tibet, while the Soviets, at least in the end, recognized the greater American interest in Cuba. One of the great difficulties involved in the Vietnam clash has been the inability to determine whose interests are greater and who has more at stake.

While the interests and intentions of the superpowers are likely to be important determinants of the outcome of any local conflict, of perhaps equal importance will be the nature of the local situation and the local political and military balance. Some wars, of course, start and end because of local conditions; and the superpowers never become involved. As was indicated in Chapter One, this has become less and less frequent in the postwar period. Even wars which later turn out to be major confrontations between the United States, China, and the Soviet Union frequently begin because of local conditions and local pressures. The various conflicts in Vietnam and Laos, for example, were the result of pressures within Vietnam—some of them emanating from the Indochinese Communist party, but others, such as conflicts in Laos in 1962–63, apparently resulting from the restlessness of neutralists under the leadership of Captain Kong Le. Other local conflicts erupt from the deliberate decision of leaders in Peking or Moscow. This appears to have happened in the Korean War and in various crises in the Taiwan Straits. Finally, we cannot exclude the possibility of the launching of a local war by the United States or another Western power, as was the case in the Suez crisis of 1956.

We are concerned about local wars partly because the outcomes of these wars may themselves have important consequences for the future of international politics but also because of the possibility that a local war may turn into a general nuclear war. The term frequently used to express this danger is "escalation," which has now "escalated" into everyday vocabulary from the more technical vocabulary of the strategic analyst. It is important to note, however, that the term "escalation" is ambiguous and refers actually to two different processes that may come about as a local war grows in size. The first of these, which we will term *explosion*, involves the sudden occurrence of general nuclear war during the local war. This explosion into general nuclear war can take place at any time during a local war situation, even if the local war appears to be at a very low level. However, it is more likely to occur after *expansion* (the second process implied by the term "escalation") of the local war; that is, the growth in size of a local war. This expansion may be deplored or applauded precisely because it increases the danger of general nuclear war: one side may want to show its determination by engaging in action that consequently increases the risk of an explosion into general war.

An expansion of a local war may also be aimed at influencing the outcome of a local military battle.

MAJOR MILITARY PROBLEMS

We have attempted thus far in this chapter to describe a basic framework for analyzing contemporary strategic problems. With an emphasis on policy, we will use this framework to look at the major military problems facing the United States. These may be considered in terms of deterring and fighting a general nuclear war and deterring and fighting in local areas, first in Europe and then in the rest of the world. An attempt will be made here to provide an overview. Later in the book we will return to each of the problems raised in this chapter.

General Nuclear War

The major emphasis of American military policy in the postwar period has been on the deterrence of a general nuclear war between the United States and the Soviet Union. The United States tries to be in a position (referred to by the Pentagon as having "assured destruction capability") in which it can deter both deliberate attack and inadvertent general war while at the same time use its strategic forces to monitor and contain local wars. However, despite the emphasis on deterrence, some attention has been paid to what would happen if a general nuclear war did take place. Particularly in recent years we have been concerned with limiting damage to the United States in the event of a general nuclear war. In fact, recent statements by American Secretary of Defense Robert McNamara have emphasized the objectives of deterring a deliberate attack and of limiting damage in the event that a nuclear war should occur. In addition to limiting damage, some thought has been given to securing the best outcome for the United States in a general nuclear war. While some analysts, particularly within the American Air Force, have stressed the need to "win" a nuclear war, it has appeared to most of those who have examined general nuclear war that it would be impossible to "win" such a war in anything like the traditional sense of the term. The destruction in the United States would be so great that any pre-nuclear analyst would conclude that the enemy had won the war. However, it is clear that one side may come out significantly stronger than the other, both in existing military capability and in the ability to recuperate.

There may well be, at least in certain times, some conflict between efforts to deter a nuclear war and efforts to limit damage and secure the best outcome if a war should occur. It has been argued, for example, that the best form of deterrence of a deliberate attack is the threat of the greatest amount of destruction possible. However, such threats may make it more difficult to limit damage in the event of general nuclear war. Whether such conflict exists depends on the details of the technology and the attitudes of the leadership on both sides in any particular historical period. However, it appears that there has been more serious disparity between steps that would deter a deliberate attack and those that would make less likely an inadvertent general war. For example, improvements in command and control make accidental events and inadvertent war less likely; but they also make it easier for the enemy to believe that he can, by destroying the command and control systems, carry out a successful first strike.

In seeking to develop a proper policy for deterring and, if necessary, fighting a general nuclear war, several alternative strategies have been considered by the American government and by private analysts. Any military strategy dealing with any particular policy problem can be considered in terms of three components:

1. *Capability.* What hardware of various kinds—what missiles and airplanes, for example—a country should buy, with what characteristics, how many of them with what air bases, what systems for communicating with strategic forces, and so on.

2. *Communication.* What it is that the leadership of a country wants its enemy to believe about how it will use the strategic forces it has deployed. There is much less control over communications than over capabilities; however, the leadership of any country can, and frequently does, have an explicit policy of what it wants the enemy to believe. How to make the enemy believe this, amidst much conflicting information from other sources both within the country and outside it, is a complex policy problem. In addition to what the leadership of a country says, the capabilities

of a country, as well as its past and present action, influence the enemy's credibility of that country's intentions.

3. *Action.* The actual plans for employing the military capability in any given circumstances. In attempting to evaluate an historical strategy, we can identify the action policy of a country; looking to the future, we can only talk about what the country thinks it will do in a given situation.

In terms of these categories, three strategies that deal with the problem of deterring or fighting a general nuclear war can be identified. These are *minimum deterrence, controlled response,* and *credible first strike.*

When a country employs a strategy of minimum deterrence it uses a relatively small strategic force to attack enemy population centers in order to convince the enemy that it will only use the force in retaliation for an enemy first strike. The strategic forces are used, if at all, in a second strike; very little concern is given to the actual fighting of a general nuclear war.

The strategy of controlled response, which appears to resemble closely current American policy, calls for a relatively large strategic force—perhaps about two thousand strategic delivery vehicles, with very good command and control systems—and the ability to use this strategic force in controlled, limited, and precise ways. A country using this strategy tries to convince its opponent that it will not use strategic forces except by careful and deliberate decision and that if it does employ strategic forces, it will be in a limited and controlled way, perhaps only against strategic forces. This strategy suggests that a first strike might be launched in return for major provocation, for example, a Soviet attack on West Germany (or, in the terminology used by NATO, on the central front in Europe). Great emphasis is placed not only on deterring a general nuclear war but also on limiting damage in the event that such a war were to occur.

The strategy of a credible first strike, which demonstrates the role that strategic forces play in influencing the outcome of a local war, calls for the development of a very large strategic force—two or three times more than that called for by a controlled-response strategy—capable of destroying most of the enemy's strategic forces. By using the strategy of a credible first strike, a country would convey to its enemy that there is a significant probability that a first strike will be launched in the event of various kinds of provocation. In the event of war, this strategy prescribes a very large first strike directed at all of the enemy's strategic forces.

These three alternatives raise a number of specific issues, which can be considered in terms of capability, communication, and action.

A major issue of American defense policy in the postwar period has been: How much of a strategic force is enough? Or, as the critics of current policy put it: How much "overkill" do we need? Some analysts have suggested that a very small strategic force, perhaps one hundred intercontinental missiles, is sufficient; at the other extreme, some have argued that the United States should produce as many strategic forces as it can. The decisions in between are much more complicated. This debate has most recently taken the form of how much damage-limiting capability to buy; that is, how much the United States should spend on strategic offensive forces, air and missile defense forces, and civil defense to reduce expected casualties in the event of nuclear war.

In the last several years it has become clear that just as important as the quantity of the strategic forces is the quality of those forces: their accuracy and their ability to survive an enemy attack, to penetrate enemy defenses, and to be used in controlled and sophisticated ways. The reaction time of the forces may also be important; in the last several years the decrease in reaction time has been significant. Bombers may take from six to eight hours to reach their target; liquid-fuel missiles took perhaps an hour to be readied for firing and then a half hour to reach their targets; solid-fuel missiles can be fired in a matter of seconds and can reach their target in less than a half hour. Since 1960 the United States—and apparently to some extent the Soviet Union—has spent very large sums of money improving the quality of strategic forces—improving, in particular, command and control systems, and the ability to use the force in sophisticated and selective ways.

American communication policy about general nuclear war has been ambiguous throughout the postwar period. On the one hand, American officials emphasize the traditional American reluctance to begin a general nuclear war and state that the United States would never be the "aggressor." On the other hand, it is clear that American policy for the defense of Europe includes the threat to launch a nuclear attack on the Soviet Union in response to a Soviet attack in Europe.

A second major issue in the communication field has been what sort of attack the United States should threaten to launch. The question here has been whether the United States should indicate that it will bomb cities as well as strategic forces. As will be further discussed in Chapter Seven, the United States in the last several years has stated that it might not strike Soviet cities, particularly if the Soviet Union refrained from attacking American cities. The Soviets, on the other hand, have stressed that they would strike cities as well as strategic forces in the event of a nuclear war.

Deterrence of a deliberate attack would appear to be strengthened by emphasis on the hair-trigger nature of, or loosely controlled, strategic forces; since, if strategic forces are only loosely controlled, they can more readily react to early signs of an enemy attack and, consequently, are less likely to be destroyed. On the contrary, however, American communication policy has stressed that American strategic forces are under tight command and control, would not be used in provocative ways, and would not be launched except in the case of clear evidence of a Soviet attack.

There has been considerable reluctance in the United States and elsewhere to think about what would occur in the event of general nuclear war. Since the development of an American atomic arsenal, military planners have produced plans for the employment of nuclear weapons, should they be ordered into use by the President. However, it is only in the last several years, and particularly since the publication of Herman Kahn's monumental work, *On Thermonuclear War*, that attention has been given to how a general nuclear war should be conducted.

A major question, which now appears to have been settled, is whether or not the United States should contemplate inadvertent nuclear war. American leaders apparently have enough confidence in the ability of United States' strategic forces to survive a Soviet first strike that they are determined to be sure that the strike has occurred, by waiting for a significant number of missiles to hit the United States, before launching American forces. In this way, American forces would not be triggered by "geese on the radar screen," the accidental firing of a few Soviet missiles, or an attempt by a local Soviet commander or a third country to simulate an all-out Soviet attack. Although the United States has retained the option of striking first in response to massive Soviet aggression in Europe, it has emphasized the desire not to be faced by this dilemma, by increasing its own ability to respond to Soviet aggression in kind or at levels below a general nuclear strike.

Perhaps the most significant question that would face the United States in the event of a nuclear war would be how large a strike to employ. If American action were in response to a Soviet strike, the magnitude of the strike would very likely be influenced by the nature of the Soviet attack. At one extreme, the United States might launch all of its strategic forces against military targets and population centers in the Soviet Union and China. At the other extreme, it would launch a very limited strike against a few targets in the Soviet Union, withholding the great bulk of its force to threaten city destruction. In the 1950's American strategy seemed to call for the destruction of Soviet cities as quickly as possible in the event of war. From this perspective one talked about the "bonus damage" received from attacking strategic targets: the United States would get added value from an attack in which a weapon, which struck on an airbase, would through its fallout or blast kill a large number of civilians, since destruction in the Soviet Union would be increased. Another approach to city damage is essentially to ignore it; that is, to launch strategic forces against Soviet military installations without reference to whether or not this brings on large-scale civilian destruction, neither desiring civilian destruction nor taking any steps to avoid it. A third approach, and one that seems to influence current American policy, suggests launching a sizable attack against strategic forces but avoiding city damage.

The withholding of strategic forces that could be used in city destruction rests on the belief that deterrence can continue even after general nuclear war begins. It is assumed that there will be communication, perhaps on the so-called "hot line" between Moscow and Washington, and also that both sides will communicate by the way in which they use their strategic forces. Since we need to communicate only if we want to negotiate an end to the war, communication would suggest a willingness to stop the war short of the all-out use of strategic forces, combined with a threat to attack cities if the war continues. The problem of how to terminate a general nuclear war is one that has been given very little attention in the United States, but it is a question that is likely to receive greater interest over the next several years.

THE DEFENSE OF LOCAL AREAS

If the deterrence of general nuclear war has received the most attention in the United States, it is not because it has been viewed as the most likely military threat, but rather because it is seen as the most serious threat—one that could cause destruction of American civilization. It has been recognized, however, that local threats in the NATO area and beyond it are much more likely. Such threats have taken in the past, and could in the future take, three basic forms: nuclear blackmail, conventional attack, and subversion.

In trying to deal with threats of local aggression, the United States has at least in principle a series of options. First, it can hope that local forces themselves will be sufficient to deal with the threat. Secondly, it can depend on its own or alliance ground forces. Finally, it can try to use strategic nuclear forces.

As was emphasized earlier in this chapter, there are many causes of local aggression. For this reason, and because in many areas of the world no acceptable substitute for violence as a means of political change has developed, much more attention has been given to actually fighting, rather than simply deterring, local wars. A variety of strategies have been proposed for this purpose, mainly with relevance to NATO, but also for the defense of countries in the third world of Asia, Africa, and Latin America. These will be outlined briefly here and considered in greater detail in discussing problems of defense in the NATO area and in the Far East (in Chapters Nine and Ten). The alternatives that have been suggested are massive retaliation, limited retaliation, the use of alliance strategic nuclear forces, use of national strategic nuclear forces, and direct defense with or without nuclear weapons.

The strategy of massive retaliation holds that the forces which are sufficient to deter a Soviet nuclear strike on the United States also are sufficient to deter or defeat any lesser form of Communist aggression. The strategy suggests that the United States needs very little beyond its strategic nuclear capabilities and that it should threaten to conduct a first strike in the event of Communist aggression. This capability is viewed as adequate to deter any Soviet or Chinese move. It calls for the credible-first-strike capability discussed earlier in this chapter.

A second strategy, which depends at least in part on the use of strategic forces, is that of limited retaliation. As will be discussed in Chapter Four, it is the policy implied by Secretary of State Dulles in his famous "massive retaliation" speech. This strategy calls for the limited use of strategic forces to deter or defeat local aggression, and proposes that the United States communicate to its opponents that it will not deal with aggression on the level on which it occurs but rather will feel free to respond with nuclear weapons against strategic targets in the homeland of China or of the Soviet Union.

The strategies of massive and limited retaliation, as outlined above, are based on the employment of American strategic forces. Both of these lines of action might also be implemented by alliance nuclear forces or by the national nuclear forces possessed by the country attacked.

Strategies that employ strategic forces—whether controlled by the United States or its allies—in order to defend local areas against direct attack, also call for some ground forces, at least for the purpose of establishing the fact that aggression has taken place. The enemy would have to attack and destroy the existing ground forces, leaving no doubt that aggression had occurred. Within the last several years the limits of the use of strategic nuclear forces in deterring various kinds of aggression, particularly those involving political pressure or guerrilla warfare, have become increasingly evident; and attention has been focused on direct defense. The two central issues that evolve here are: Should the United States commit its own forces or rely on indigenous forces, and should the United States use a tactical nuclear weapon strategy or a conventional strategy in the defense of particular areas.

Again, these alternative strategies have raised a number of specific issues, which can be considered in terms of capability, communication, and action.

In terms of capability, the quantity of American forces necessary has produced among others, two difficult problems: How large a conventional war should the United States fight before introducing nuclear weapons, and should the United States be prepared to fight two or more limited wars at the same time.

The relative capability of fighting with or without nuclear weapons has raised unsolved problems. There is not yet any clear notion of how a tactical nuclear war should or would be fought and no decisive way to choose between a force capable of fighting conventionally and one capable of fighting with tactical nuclear weapons. The American Army has vacillated between trying to design its divisions specifically for nuclear war and then adding on the capability for conventional action and, at the other extreme, developing forces to fight conventionally and then adding on a tactical nuclear capability. The problem of producing a new capability for both tactical nuclear warfare and conventional action remains perhaps the most important problem requiring analysis and clarification.

A subsidiary issue concerns the extent of sea- and air-lift capability needed. One of the major changes brought about by the McNamara Administration in the Pentagon was a very substantial increase in American air- and sea-lift capability, which would enable the United States to move several divisions anywhere in the world within a very short time. The relative merits of stationing divisions in the field, planning to fly in troops and equipment, or pre-positioning some equipment and then flying in the troops are difficult to calculate.

Communication policy for a local war is exceedingly difficult to specify in the abstract. The United States has been faced with the problem in several locations and has had to decide whether or not to threaten intervention and, if so, how ambiguous to be about the threat. Another question has been whether to threaten intervention with or without the use of nuclear weapons. The same problems exist with determining action policies: When should the United States intervene and when should it use nuclear weapons?

It should be clear that the creation of modern weapons has

posed a series of formidable and novel problems, both for the strategic analyst and for American and Soviet policymakers. Considerable effort has been given to developing techniques, particularly quantitative ones, for dealing with these problems. In the next chapter, we consider some of these techniques and their limitations.

SELECTED BIBLIOGRAPHY

Aron, Raymond. *The Great Debate*. Garden City: Doubleday & Co., 1965.

Brown, Neville. *Nuclear War: The Impending Strategic Deadlock*. London: Pall Mall, 1964.

The Military Balance. Annual publication of the Institute for Strategic Studies, London.

Quester, George. *Deterrence Before Hiroshima*. New York: John Wiley & Sons, 1966.

Schelling, Thomas C. *The Strategy of Conflict*. Cambridge, Mass.: Harvard University Press, 1960.

Statement by Secretary of Defense to House and Senate Armed Services Committees (annually); available in the Budget Hearings of the House and Senate Armed Services Committees.

CHAPTER THREE

Qualitative and Quantitative
Research Methods

Military strategy may be viewed, as it is in this book, as an aspect of the role of force in international politics. However, strategic questions have also been studied in the postwar period from several other vantage points. A policy perspective has been adopted within the government and also in private research institutes such as the RAND Corporation. Should the United States deploy medium-range missiles in Europe? What threats should have been made during the Cuban missile crisis? What action should have been taken during the Berlin blockade? Questions such as these have been subjected to systematic analysis.

Others have seen military strategy as an aspect of a broader theoretical interest. For example, for some economists, military-strategy decisions are part of the problem of the allocation of scarce resources. For some game theorists—those who study the mathematical theory of games—military strategy has proven to be a fertile field for examples of competitive and cooperative interaction. Others with a general interest in "conflict" theory have looked to military questions for insights and applications.

This chapter will seek to examine the *quantitative methods*— that is, the use of mathematics and statistics—which have been employed in the study of military strategy, to assess their limitations, and to explore the ways in which quantitative methods can be combined with *qualitative methods*—those which do not employ numbers.

QUANTITATIVE METHODS

There are two basic quantitative methods that have been introduced into the study of military strategy. Within the framework of these two methods a number of specific quantitative techniques have been suggested. The first method is known as systems analysis: an attempt to assess the effectiveness of a military weapon as a complete system in operation over a period of time against an opponent who calculates what his enemy may do. The techniques of systems analysis are used, for example, to calculate the possible outcome of a general nuclear war and to assess the effect, on the likely outcome of the war, of new weapons systems or new strategies used in existing systems. One systems study done for the government on a classified basis in the early 1950's and publicly released in the 1960's examined the role of overseas bases in American strategic foreign policy. It drew on a variety of quantitative techniques to assess the most efficient way of using existing American bombers and those to be procured. The study examined possible combinations of American and overseas bases and recommended what was considered to be optimum deployment of planes on bases. Systems-analysis studies relate to situations in which there are competing objectives. Where there is only one objective —for example, to destroy enemy submarines—the techniques employed are called operations analysis.

The second method—one frequently used in conjunction with systems analysis—is that of cost-effectiveness comparative analysis. It seeks to compare the cost of using two different methods to secure a particular objective or, alternatively, the relative effectiveness of two systems having approximately the same cost. This technique involves looking not only at the cost of buying particular hardware but also at the five-year operating cost of the military equipment being purchased. This method frequently employs concepts from economics, such as marginal utility.

The techniques of systems analysis and cost effectiveness have been used increasingly in the Pentagon since Robert S. McNamara became the Secretary of Defense in 1961. Much of this analysis is done on a classified basis, but there are also some unclassified studies. By briefly examining a few examples, we should be able to understand the techniques and also the value of using them—even if only with illustrative numbers—in comprehending the nature of the problem. Moreover, it is held that relatively accurate data for quantitative analysis can be obtained from unclassified sources. Two illustrations should help clarify the nature of systems analysis and cost-effectiveness studies.

One study examined the desirable limits on strategic forces in a possible arms-control agreement between the United States and the Soviet Union. The study asked: What desirable constraints ought to be written into a treaty that seeks to limit strategic forces on both sides and thereby reduce the danger of an inadvertent nuclear war? The study concluded that one should put a limit on total megatonnage and on missile-site locations rather than on the number of missiles, as had frequently been suggested in qualitative analysis of the problem.

A second study asked whether or not there was a military need for the placement of missiles in Europe. This study involved essentially a cost-effectiveness analysis of the role of, for example, two hundred missiles, which might be placed in Europe, as against two hundred additional Minutemen intercontinental ballistic missiles. It compared the cost and effectiveness of these two alternatives and concluded that at any conceivable level of American strategic force, it was more desirable to add two hundred missiles to the intercontinental capability than to build a medium-range missile force.

QUALITATIVE METHODS

Even the most enthusiastic advocates of quantitative methods warn that these methods must be combined with qualitative insights in making strategic decisions. However, because of the amorphous nature of qualitative inputs, the need to add them to quantitative analysis is frequently overlooked. In fact, it is rather difficult to specify the nature of the techniques used in qualitative analysis. They involve using the lessons one has learned from history, from a general study of politics, and from a particular study of the enemies and allies with which one is dealing; but how these insights are to be used seems to defy organized analysis.

In addition to its direct role in dealing with strategic issues, qualitative analysis is also important in specifying the terms for any quantitative analysis. For example, systems analysts frequently stress the great importance of asking the right questions of the data being analyzed. Consideration of the vulnerability of strategic forces to destruction on the ground by the enemy, of the cost to the enemy of countering any action taken by its opponent, and of the five-year operating costs as well as the purchase costs of any given military equipment—these qualitative insights have drastically altered the shape of all quantitative analysis done on strategic problems in the United States in the last several years. Insights of this kind can arise, not only from qualitative analysis, but also in the process of carrying out quantitative analysis—a fact which underlines the value of even heuristic exercises.

THE INTERACTION OF QUANTITATIVE AND QUALITATIVE ANALYSES

There is little dispute that one needs to use quantitative data wherever possible, but there is also no question that if one goes beyond very narrow technical questions, quantitative data alone is not sufficient. Several interactions between qualitative and quantitative analyses in the fields of capability, communication, and action will be discussed to illustrate the process of strategic analysis.

The question of determining the optimum military capability for the United States, with a given defense budget, is in one sense a problem in the economic analysis of scarce resources. In another sense, it is a problem of dealing with a rational and responsive opponent. Three different kinds of issues, which have been important in American defense policy in the postwar period, will be considered in attempting to illustrate the roles of qualitative and quantitative analyses in the assessment of decisions about military capability.

The first of these concerns the role of strategic forces. Involved in making decisions is asking the right questions; that is, developing the right qualitative insights about what the issues really are.

One essential question is: How vulnerable are various systems to an enemy strategic first strike? Another concerns the goals desired from using strategic forces: Is deterrence alone the goal? Is limiting damage, if war occurs, a concern? Is it important to win the war in some sense? Finally, are strategic forces to be used for other purposes than deterring or fighting a general nuclear war? In order to answer such questions, we need detailed quantitative analyses of the costs of accomplishing various objectives. Systems analyses combining the operation of a variety of strategic offensive and defensive systems are required. The cost of obtaining a certain probability of destroying a given target is a valid concern; so is the decrease in casualties in the United States, if the Soviet Union can be induced not to attack American cities.

Thus quantitative analysis is important and necessary but does not come close to providing a complete answer. What we need to know is the enemy's calculations—not our own calculations—of under what circumstances we will attack, for his calculations may be very different for a variety of reasons. Thus, if we are most interested in strategic forces because of their role in deterring the enemy's use of strategic forces, our most important calculations will be what, in fact, will deter the enemy; this is not necessarily the same as what will actually work most effectively should a war occur.

In addition, in determining the role of strategic forces, we are likely to discover important conflicts between various values. For example (as was indicated in Chapter Two), one strategic posture may look better in terms of deterring an inadvertent attack, another more efficient in terms of deterring a deliberate attack, and a third most effective in limiting damage, should war occur. Conflicts may also arise between objectives in the field of strategic weapons and other objectives in, as well as outside, the defense field. Even if we could determine exactly how much deterrence we could buy for any given sum of money, the question of whether that much deterrence is worth buying could only be judged in relation to what else we could buy with that money.

Finally, the domestic, political, and social costs of any strategic posture must be assessed. For example, most of the objection to civil defense—whether justified or not—has been on the basis of its effect on political and social life in the United States: the belief that a civil defense program would create conflicts between the rich, who could afford their own shelters, and the poor, who could not.

At the highest level of generalization, quantitative analysis is extremely complicated and difficult to perform; it plays a vital, but limited, role in strategic analysis. However, the more limited the kinds of decisions are, the greater the role of quantitative methods.

A more limited kind of decision about military capability would be whether or not the United States should buy a new bomber; consequently, the role of quantitative analysis in determining this problem is greater than in evaluating the role of strategic forces. The question is primarily one of cost effectiveness: comparing any new manned bomber with other systems in relation to their ability both to limit damage, if war should occur, and to deter a nuclear war in the context of any given strategy.

The first objective—limiting damage if war occurs—is a straightforward quantitative problem, except for uncertainties, such as how good the enemy defense is and how well the pilot can fly. Given the goal of reducing damage in a certain kind of general nuclear war, the relative effectiveness of a particular bomber, as opposed to other strategic systems, is easy to determine.

The deterrent role of bombers, on the other hand, is more difficult to determine. It is impossible to quantify the role of bombers in deterrence beyond restating the cost effectiveness of the bombers. As was stressed above, however, the more relevant calculation may be the Soviet estimate of cost effectiveness and beyond that the psychological impact of the existence, or absence, of bombers on the American strategic force.

Finally, other values within the American economy—for example, building the Great Society and reducing draft calls—can, and legitimately do, come into play in deciding whether or not to produce any given weapons system.

Our third illustration of a capability decision is a local-war problem; it poses the question of how to spend funds efficiently for American ground troops. For a variety of historical reasons—including the fact that the RAND Corporation, which has been the pioneer in quantitative techniques, has done most of its work for the Air Force—there has been much less quantitative work done on local-war problems. Moreover, such problems are much less susceptible to systematic quantitative analysis. There are, however, three alternatives, which could be used in combination, for deploying military forces so that they would be effective in any particular spot on the globe. The first alternative is to keep all forces and their equipment in the United States and spend large sums of money on air- and sea-lift capability. At the other extreme is the second alternative: to try to station the forces in the area in which military conflict is anticipated. A third alternative is to pre-position heavy equipment in the areas of likely conflict and to station the troops and their light equipment, with extensive airlift capability, in the United States.

Clearly, there are important quantitative aspects to this problem. In one sense, it is simply a problem of operations analysis; that is, systems analysis in which there are no conflicting objectives, the only objective being to get the most men with a given combat efficiency to the most areas at the least cost. But considering, for example, the real issue of decreasing the number of American troops stationed in Europe and, instead, pre-positioning equipment in Europe, with increased airlift capabilities for the central reserve in the United States, we realize that political considerations—which cannot be quantified—can dominate the problem. In this case, perhaps the most important political consideration is the German belief that the more American troops there are in Europe, the more likely it is that the United States will fight to defend Germany.

The deterrence of local war is perhaps even more complicated than the deterrence of a Soviet nuclear strike. Here again we have to deal with both inadvertent and deliberate aggression but also with aggression from a variety of different parties and the possibility of a spontaneous outbreak of violence. It is almost impossible to specify, for the deterrence of any given action or possible combination of actions, the relative effectiveness of five divisions on the ground in Europe or two divisions and the equipment for three more divisions, which could be flown in within two weeks.

In the postwar period, the number of American ground troops in Europe has had a significant effect on alliance relations; consequently, this effect has been an important factor in determining the number of ground troops to be maintained. The United States has kept a large army in Europe for the purpose of reinforcing the credibility that it would use its strategic nuclear forces—if necessary—to defeat Soviet aggression. During the early postwar period these forces also provided a suitable framework for an acceptable rearmament of Germany; they are now important in demonstrating an American political commitment to Europe. None of these objectives are easy to quantify, and whatever qualifications would be involved would not be directly related to the military capability of the forces.[1]

If, as we have stressed, the role of quantitative analysis is of important, but only limited, value in the study of capability requirements, it is even of less value in the study of communication and action policies. Perhaps the main role of quantitative analysis in devising an effective communication policy is determining the possible credibility of a statement.

To choose an example from the local-war area, there is much discussion about whether or not the United States should convince the Soviet Union that it is willing to fight a conventional war in Europe. There is an important quantitative issue here; namely, the cost of deploying conventional defense forces capable of defeating a Soviet conventional attack of a given magnitude. But many uncertainties exist—both in the data and in the methods to be used. For example, the size of the Soviet force in Europe is ambiguous to intelligence specialists. Moreover, how to compute the effectiveness of these ground forces and the likely outcome of a ground battle remains extremely unclear.

All of these questions are overshadowed in importance by one question: What actions are the NATO governments willing and able to take? If, for example, Europeans believe that an increase in conventional capability decreases deterrence and they believe this because of judgments about Soviet attitudes, no amount of quantitative debate about the cost of the conventional capabilities will change their position. By the same token, if governments agree that conventional forces would improve deterrence but feel

[1] The behaviorally oriented political scientist will recognize that the focus of this chapter is on quantitative methods uniquely related to problems of military strategy. Many of the problems described here as "qualitative" could be subjected to at least partial quantitative analysis by techniques used by behavioral scientists.

that the money is better spent on housing or world economic developments, the quantitative data is of limited value.

The debate about whether or not the United States should communicate to the Soviets that a nuclear war might be fought without attacking cities in the early stages of the war, reveals the same relatively limited role for quantitative analysis. Here, again, there is an extremely important quantitative question: What would the decrease in casualties in the United States, the Soviet Union, and Western Europe be if the attacks by both sides were directed only at strategic targets and not at cities? But, as has already been indicated, we have to go beyond that question and ask other questions about the effect of deterrence on the arms race and on our alliance relationships—questions that, at least so far, have defied quantitative analysis.

When we turn to action policies, the complications in analysis become even more pronounced; and the emphasis has tended to be on providing the decision-maker with options and flexibility so that he can respond wisely to a variety of situations. However, it may become important in some situations to assess the probable outcome of a military conflict in order to determine the proper action policy.

Assessing the probable outcome was important during the Cuban missile crisis of 1962. One of the many questions facing American decision-makers at that time was how valuable missiles in Cuba would be to the Soviet Union in case of a war. Here the systems analysis was relatively complicated; it posed several different questions: Who would strike first, the Soviet Union or the United States? Would the war begin after an alert of the strategic forces? What was the cost and the feasibility of an airborne alert for bombers for the purpose of reducing their vulnerability to Soviet missiles in Cuba? By ignoring the great uncertainties involved, it was possible to produce quantitative answers about the effect on various war outcomes of Soviet placement of a given number of missiles in Cuba.

The effect on the course of international politics or even on the outcome of a general nuclear war was a much more difficult problem to analyze. For example, the calculations assumed that a war with strategic-force targets was relevant either because it might occur or because, if it did occur, it would affect political decisions.

However, it is by no means clear that these assumptions were valid. Moreover, what appeared to be important were perceptions on both sides about how the Soviet move would change the strategic balance. Most political analysts—not to speak of politicians and the general public—tended to discuss this question in completely qualitative terms, arguing that Soviet missiles in Cuba would "drastically alter" or "tip" the strategic balance, and to discount the quantitative factors. However, it is important to note that since a country is concerned with effects on other governments and other peoples, it does no good to say that these countries *should* take the *quantitative* factors into account: we must live with qualitative political judgments. In fact, perceptions of the effect on the strategic balance were less important than the United States' image in Latin America, the likely Soviet moves in Berlin, and other political problems that may not have been closely related to the real military utility of deploying Soviet missiles in Cuba. As was the case with each of the examples discussed in this chapter, quantitative calculations were important but provided only part of the answer to any real policy question.

SELECTED BIBLIOGRAPHY

Hitch, Charles J., and Roland N. McKean. *The Economics of Defense in the Nuclear Age.* Cambridge, Mass.: Harvard University Press, 1963.

Kent, Glenn A. *On the Interaction of Opposing Forces under Possible Arms Agreements.* Harvard Center for International Affairs, Occasional Paper No. 5, March, 1963.

Quade, Edward S., ed. *Analysis for Military Decisions.* Chicago: Rand McNally & Co., 1964.

Wohlstetter, Albert, *et al. Selection and Use of Strategic Air Bases.* RAND Report, R-266, April, 1954.

CHAPTER FOUR

The Evolution of American Military Strategy

American military strategy has evolved continuously over the postwar period in response to changes in technology as well as increased sophistication in the understanding of strategic questions. This chapter will trace the evolution of American policy as well as the evolution of the analysis of strategic questions. The role of technology in shaping these evolutions will be considered.

THE EARLY POSTWAR PERIOD

During the early postwar period the United States gradually came to accept the need for a policy designed to halt the spread of Soviet communism, which threatened to engulf all of Europe. The Truman Administration accepted the containment doctrine, which argued that if Soviet expansion could be stopped, the Soviet Union would gradually lose its urge to expand. The doctrine developed from an analysis of Soviet society, and the implications of this doctrine were viewed largely in political and economic terms. The military implications of an attempt to stop Russian expansion and, consequently, the kind of military forces which might be needed over the next ten years were not given much attention.

Defense strategy in the early postwar period focused on the problem of general war, which was defined at this time as the danger of large-scale Soviet aggression in Europe. The possibility of limited local aggression, either in Europe or outside of it, was not taken seriously in war planning or force development. Very early in this period the concept of deterrence—that is, *preventing* a Soviet attack in Europe—became important. The main emphasis here was on a political commitment by the United States to defend Europe; this commitment culminated in the signing of the NATO Defense Treaty in 1949. There was a widespread belief that the Second (and even the First) World War had come about because aggressors had assumed that the United States would remain aloof and would permit them to dominate Europe. Thus, it was argued that a firm commitment in the form of the North Atlantic Treaty would be a major step toward effectively deterring a Soviet attack. Although it was recognized that the atomic bomb might potentially change all military strategy, this bomb was viewed in the postwar period simply as a somewhat bigger bomb to be used in the same way other bombs had been used at the end of the Second World War. The United States had a very small stockpile of atomic weapons, and there was no strong drive to increase to any great extent the size of the stockpile. Conventional forces were even smaller. The United States' defense budget stood at approximately fifteen billion dollars a year, and there was a popular notion in Washington that any sum larger than that would bankrupt the economy.

NSC 68 (1950)

By 1950 a number of pressures made a reevaluation of American defense policy in the Atomic Age a necessity. It had become clear that since the Cold War would last for a long time, the United States would continue to have defense commitments, which should be reevaluated in light of the growing American atomic stockpiles.

First, the Soviet Union had become a nuclear power much more quickly than anybody had expected; and the United States had decided to proceed on a top priority basis with the development of the hydrogen (fusion), or "super," bomb. This decision, made by President Truman, was one of the three immediate pressures that led to a review of American defense strategy. The second pressure came from the growing American military assistance program and the efforts of the State Department to coordinate defense and foreign policy. The tradition of separating foreign policy from military strategy made it difficult to devise an effective military assistance program; officials in the State Department, particularly Paul Nitze of the Policy Planning Staff, became aware of the need to coordinate defense and foreign policy. Finally, President Truman called on the National Security Council to take a more active role in coordinating security policy and asked the National Security Council for an appraisal of the United States' strategic situation.

These pressures led to the creation of a joint State-Defense Department committee, which was instructed to reexamine American security policy without considering either budgetary or political constraints. The committee, with the strong support of Secretary of State Dean Acheson and the active guiding role of Nitze, met for several months during 1950 and finally reported to the National Security Council in April. The report, which was endorsed by both the State Department and the Defense Department, called for a very substantial increase in the American defense effort and warned of the danger of local wars. President Truman indicated his intention to accept the report but asked for cost estimates. These were being prepared when the Korean War broke out; and the report of the committee, NSC 68, served as a blueprint for actual rearmament.

THE KOREAN WAR

The Korean War was accompanied by a vast increase in American defense spending. The defense budget went up very rapidly and then leveled off at approximately forty billion dollars a year— almost three times the fifteen billion dollar ceiling that had been reaffirmed shortly before the war. Despite the attack in the Far East and the fighting in the Korean Peninsula, the emphasis remained on Europe. It was believed that the Korean War might even be a feint on the part of the Communists to draw American power into Asia while preparing for a Soviet move in Central

Europe. Thus, while the Korean War was going on, the American forces in NATO were built up very substantially. The decision was made to create the post of Supreme Allied Commander for Europe, and General Eisenhower was appointed to the position. In 1952 the NATO Council met in Lisbon and established goals for the buildup of NATO ground forces to a total of about seventy-five active and reserve divisions on the central front. The United States rapidly expanded its own nuclear and airpower capabilities. In defense planning during the Korean War, the United States adopted the notion of a "crisis year": that several years in the future there would be a peak period of danger for the United States; in order to prepare for war in that crisis year, excessive American defense expenditures were currently required.

THE NEW LOOK

The Eisenhower Administration came into office in 1953 committed not only to ending the Korean War but also to taking a "new look" at American military strategy. We can identify at least three major sources of the new approach of the Administration.

The first of these was an affinity for airpower, which strangely enough influenced both President Eisenhower—a former Army general—and Admiral Arthur William Radford, who was to become Eisenhower's first Chairman of the Joint Chiefs. The belief that airpower could be the backbone of the American military establishment stemmed from a notion that technology could somehow substitute for manpower. The United States, being short on manpower but highly advanced technologically, could be expected —it was argued—to find a solution to its military problems by relying on its strengths and deemphasizing its weaknesses. In addition, the emphasis on airpower reflected the search for a single solution to a complex problem, which characterizes the American approach to many situations.

Of perhaps equal importance in the search for a new strategy was the notion of the great equation: the belief that the security of the United States depended as much on the health of the American economy as it did on the actual weapons used in warfare and that this health resulted from keeping expenditures down. For this reason it was felt that a lower defense budget would, in the long run, contribute more to military security than a higher budget would.

Finally, an important technological innovation of the new strategy in the United States was the development of the so-called tactical nuclear weapons—nuclear weapons of low yield which might be employed on the battlefield. Breakthroughs in technology and vast increases in the American stockpile of nuclear weapons made it possible to talk about such a use of nuclear weapons.

What, then, were the characteristics of this New Look? First of all, the notion of a crisis year was discarded and was replaced by the "long haul" concept. The crisis-year notion had been used by the Truman Administration to justify very large expenditures on the grounds that they would level off and be reduced after the United States had passed the year of great crisis; the new long-haul concept, on the other hand, justified reduced expenditures on the grounds that they would be continued indefinitely. In addition, nuclear deterrence was given more attention than it had been given before. As was noted, even under the Truman Administration prior to, and during, the Korean War the greatest threat was believed to be in Europe; it was felt that this threat was best deterred by political commitments and by nuclear power. With the advent of the New Look, the dominant role of the Air Force in American strategy was also formalized. From this followed a deemphasis on ground forces—particularly on the possibility and desirability of a conventional defense. By 1954 the NATO Council had formally committed NATO to the use of tactical nuclear weapons in the event of large-scale fighting on the central front, and NATO force requirements were reduced in the belief that tactical nuclear weapons could substitute for manpower.

In comparing the New Look policy with the pre-Korean War policy of the Truman Administration, both innovations and similarities become apparent. In both periods, the need to keep the defense budget low in order to permit the growth and health of the economy was emphasized; deterrence was largely to come from the use of atomic or nuclear weapons. Nevertheless, articulation of the military doctrines inherent in United States' policy since the Second World War resulted in a major critique of this policy, leading ultimately to its drastic revision.

CRITICISM OF MASSIVE RETALIATION

In January, 1954, Secretary of State John Foster Dulles made a speech, which later was reprinted in the *Department of State Bulletin*, to the Council on Foreign Relations in New York. The speech was an attempt on Dulles' part to explain and to justify the New Look policy of the Administration—particularly the Administration's reluctance to engage in renewed ground combat in Asia. In his talk, Dulles declared that no local defense could contain the manpower of the Communist world; therefore, he said, local defense must be reinforced by the threatened deterrent of massive retaliatory power. The United States, then, could deter local aggression by maintaining a great capacity to retaliate instantly "by means and in places of our own choosing." Dulles' formal statement of what, in reality, had long been the policy of the Administration provoked a storm of criticism, not only from leading Democrats, but also from a number of students of national security policy. These critics, who included Chester Bowles and Dean Acheson, as well as such academics as William Kaufmann and Henry Kissinger, argued that the doctrine of massive retaliation would not be effective in deterring local, more ambiguous Communist moves. They contended that massive retaliation could not be the action policy of the United States because to implement a doctrine of massive retaliation would be suicidal. Therefore, they concluded, a local-war strategy for the defense of those areas outside of Europe was needed. At least at this stage most critics of the massive-retaliation doctrine did not question its validity in Europe; only in the late 1950's and early 1960's was it felt that a direct defense strategy was essential for Europe also.

As has already been indicated, Dulles' statement was not a major change in policy, certainly not from earlier formulations of the New Look, and not even from the policy of the Truman Administration. Neither was it clear that the policy should be interpreted—as its critics suggested—as one which warned that the United States would bomb Moscow in the event of an attack by Communist forces anywhere in the world. On the contrary, the doctrine might well be interpreted as a form of limited retaliation: that the United States would not necessarily meet ground action where it occurred but might respond—with or without nuclear weapons—with attacks on strategic targets, perhaps in the Soviet Union, perhaps only in Communist China and other Communist states. There seems to be little doubt that the option of limited-retaliation, and even massive-retaliation, strategy is desirable in that it contributes to general deterrence. Even more specifically, it is now believed that Dulles' threats did enhance American deterrence of Chinese action in the Far East.

Moreover, the assumption implicit in most of the criticism was that there was inherently a stable nuclear balance between the United States and the Soviet Union: that nuclear war was very unlikely and was deterred simply by each side's having nuclear weapons. There was little regard for the vulnerability of these weapons to an enemy attack; rather, it was believed that nuclear war would consist primarily of attacks on cities. It was this image that enabled Dulles' critics to say that if he was threating Moscow, he had to accept in return the threat of New York's destruction. In fact, in 1954 and for several years after, both the United States and the Soviet Union could have destroyed, in a strategic first strike, much of their enemy's capacity to retaliate. It was not until several years later that critics outside the government began to warn that the Administration was not only overlooking the need for large ground forces but also the need for well-protected strategic forces.

Finally, it should be noted that at least some of the issues between Dulles and his critics were quantitative ones that had been expressed qualitatively. Dulles recognized and accepted the need for local-war forces; he argued, however, that by themselves they would never be large enough to contain communism and therefore had to be supplemented by nuclear power. His critics presumably were contending that larger forces could—and should —be supplied and that these forces might at least in some circumstances be sufficient to deter or defeat a Communist attack. The real issue, then, was the size of the American ground forces, not what they should be used for.

In the long run, the critics of the massive-retaliation doctrine made their impact on the intellectual climate and defense thinking in the United States. This influence culminated in 1961, when a number of these critics were brought into power with the Kennedy Administration. The effect on policy during the remaining years of the Eisenhower Administration, however, was to be much less dramatic. The criticisms did slowly bring about a few changes, though. The need for larger ground forces—at least for tactical nuclear ground defense—was accepted. Finally, the need for a limited-war strategy—albeit a nuclear one—was acknowledged in 1957, when the trend of thinking was suddenly reversed by events in the latter part of that year.

SPUTNIK AND THE GAITHER COMMITTEE

In October, 1957 the first artificial earth satellite—the Soviet Sputnik—was launched into the sky, creating the impression of Soviet superiority, not only in technology, but also in military capability. This event dramatically turned attention to the Soviet nuclear threat to the United States and, consequently, turned it away from the more remote threat of local war. It generated a climate in which increases in the American defense budget were possible; but the increases were to be for counteracting the impending Soviet ICBM capability, which threatened the United States with destruction.

If Sputnik provided the emotional impetus for a fresh appraisal of the direct defense of the United States, the Gaither Committee provided the intellectual support.

The Gaither Committee was appointed by President Eisenhower early in 1957 to consider a proposal for an extensive fallout-shelter program in the United States. The Committee was comprised of private citizens, many of whom had served under President Truman and were later to serve during the Kennedy and Johnson Administrations. They included William C. Foster, who was to become Director of the Arms Control and Disarmament Agency, and Jerome Wiesner, who later served as science advisor to President Kennedy. This group, like the committee which drew up NSC 68, was neither bound by current strategy nor by a budget ceiling. In its report, which was presented to the President and the National Security Council shortly after the launching of Sputnik, the Committee warned, for the first time, of the danger of a "missile gap." It stated that unless the United States stepped up its program of intercontinental strategic force, the

Soviet Union would have a larger strategic force and, moreover, would have the capability in a first strike of destroying all of the American strategic capability. The Committee thus urged a substantial increase in the defense budget, aimed primarily at improving the American strategic posture. The report of the Committee, which has never been formally released, made recommendations very similar to those of an unclassified study that was part of the Rockefeller Brothers Fund report on the United States at mid-century. These recommendations, coupled with the impact of Sputnik, led to a slight increase in the defense budget; the shift to a greater emphasis on local defense forces was never realized. Perhaps most important, the Gaither episode demonstrated the inability of any group, either in opposition to the President or comprised mainly of private citizens (or, as in this case, both), to influence military strategy. However, the Committee—largely because many of its findings were leaked to the press—did provoke the missile-gap debate.

The reports of both the Gaither Committee and the Rockefeller Brothers Fund were influenced by a revolution that was taking place in strategic analysis in the United States. The assumption of previous thinking had been that the strategic balance was in some way inherently stable. An image of the nuclear powers as scorpions in a bottle who could sting each other to death but only at the price of being stung to death in return, prevailed. Most of the intellectual basis for revising this image was taken from the work of Albert Wohlstetter, of the RAND Corporation. The most systematic public statement of the position was made by Wohlstetter in an article entitled "The Delicate Balance of Terror," in the January, 1959 issue of *Foreign Affairs*. Wohlstetter said that by attacking its enemy's strategic forces, a country could disarm the other "scorpion" and not be stung back. This position stressed the importance of second-strike forces; that is, forces which could survive a first strike and could retaliate. It maintained that a country should assess the vulnerability of its forces to a counterforce first strike and then should develop well-protected second-strike forces, using such techniques as hardening, dispersal, and airborne or ground alert. This view, which has not been generally accepted within the defense community, implied that there was no inherent stable balance, but rather that a country had to spend a good deal of money—including resources for research, development, communications, and control systems—to build up a credible deterrent against a determined opponent with an efficient first-strike capability. This position, in suggesting that even for the long run a significant portion of American spending would have to be on strategic forces, had important implications for the allocation of defense resources.

1960 ELECTION

Defense issues played an important part in the 1960 presidential campaign between John F. Kennedy and Richard Nixon. Nixon, while feeling obliged to defend the Administration, did suggest that larger spending would be necessary. Kennedy launched a full-scale attack on the Administration's defense posture, criticizing its effort both in the strategic field and in the field of conventional forces. He warned of the danger of a missile gap, which would permit the Soviets to have a larger strategic force—one perhaps capable of destroying the American force in a coordinated first strike—than the United States. Although this charge was clearly made in good faith, there apparently never was any real danger of a missile gap or a deterrence gap. Kennedy also suggested—more accurately—that the United States had seriously neglected conventional forces and an air- and sea-lift capability for them. He expressed the need for having the option to fight without the use of nuclear weapons.

THE MCNAMARA PENTAGON

Secretary of Defense Robert S. McNamara has been responsible for very significant changes in both the substance and the method of formulating American defense policy. Three basic sources of the changes brought about by McNamara, with the support of President Kennedy and later President Johnson, can be identified. The first of these was an intellectual one. During the 1950's a growing discontent with the massive-retaliation policy of the Eisenhower Administration was perceptible. Much work was being done in the universities, in private research corporations such as

RAND, and by the Democratic party through the Democratic Advisory Committee, on alternative approaches to both the content and the method of formulating defense policy. In addition, because defense had become one of the campaign issues Kennedy used to challenge the Eisenhower Administration, sweeping changes were needed to justify the use of this issue. Of great importance was the attitude of the new Administration toward economic questions. Kennedy's economic advisers believed that the threat to the American economy—and what, in fact, explained its sluggish growth rate during the 1950's—was the Administration's reluctance to spend money. They felt that the economy could afford, and would be stimulated by, increases in defense spending. Thus, while some attention was given to reduction of governmental expenditures, there was no strong pressure to keep the defense budget down in order to keep the economy strong. The removal of this constraint made it possible to realize substantial increases in the defense budget.

Breakthroughs in technology were also important in shaping the new defense strategy. Improvements in missiles made it possible for the United States to manufacture, in large numbers, sophisticated missile systems with great accuracy and low megatonnage, such as the Minuteman and Polaris submarine-launched strategic systems. In addition, the reconnaissance capability of the United States, mainly comprised of orbiting satellites, made possible the development of a strategy with much more reliable information about Soviet capability. Finally, the growing Soviet strategic capability, mainly against Europe, but also against the United States, made it necessary to re-think American defense policy.

Perhaps the most important and enduring change was in the structure of the Pentagon and in the decision-making processes. Mr. McNamara relied more on his civilian advisers than on the armed services and employed the techniques of systems analysis and cost-effectiveness analysis discussed in Chapter Three. The Administration also introduced program budgeting; that is, organizing the budget around functions. For example, budget headings such as Strategic Offensive and Defensive Forces, and General Purposes (local war) Forces were used rather than such administrative headings as Personnel, Maintenance, and Construction. In addition to the procedural changes, there were important alterations in the areas of counter-insurgency, conventional forces, and general-war doctrine.

Counter-insurgency—that is, actions to defeat guerrilla operations—received much more attention than it had in the past. Apparently President Kennedy came into office with a deep personal interest in problems of counter-insurgency; this interest was reinforced by the developing crises in Laos and Vietnam. A special school was set up for training military officers in aspects of counter-insurgency; and, at the high policy levels of the government, more study was given to the problem. However, in this area, the Administration did not have a large amount of intellectual capital to draw on; and only limited headway was made.

In the area of conventional forces, much work had been done. President Kennedy, as a senator, had been concerned with shortages in American conventional capability. Shortly after Mr. McNamara took over the Pentagon, programs that increased the size of the Army from twelve to sixteen combat divisions and stressed procurement, research, and development for conventional capability were initiated. This was the first noteworthy effort in this direction since the Second World War. The United States also began to urge its NATO allies to engage in a conventional buildup. Although the United States did develop an improved capability to fight conventionally, its action and communication policies on the relative role of conventional and nuclear forces continued to be ambiguous. It was evident, though, that the focus of statements did shift toward a greater emphasis on conventional forces. The President and the Secretary of Defense continued to stress the need for options and the need to develop a conventional capability; but they refused to be drawn into any specific discussion of when nuclear weapons would be used, except to assert that they would be used "if necessary." In the early 1960's the United States developed an increased capability to fight without the use of nuclear weapons and began to use some of that capability in Vietnam. But what the action policy would be in other parts of the world remained uncertain.

Judging by his statements during the campaign, Mr. Kennedy expected to come into office confronted with Soviet superiority in strategic weapons. Instead, he found that the United States still possessed an overwhelming strategic advantage. The Administration asserted the political value of this superiority: that it gave the United States greater freedom of political maneuver on international questions. At the same time, an increase in American strategic forces, with well-protected, accurate strategic systems and good command and control, was ordered. The United States began to develop forces that could survive a nuclear attack and sought ways to limit a general nuclear war. This led to the enunciation of the controlled-response strategy and later to the development of the assured-destruction (for deterrence) and damage-limiting (should war occur) strategies. At the same time, the Administration began to talk about allied joint nuclear planning (discussed in detail in Chapter Seven).

By the mid 1960's the McNamara revolution in the Pentagon was in a sense complete. Defense decision making was relying more and more on quantitative techniques of analysis. A series of options for meeting a wide variety of military threats had been developed.

SELECTED BIBLIOGRAPHY

Hammond, Paul Y. *Organizing for Defense*. Princeton, N.J.: Princeton University Press, 1961.

Huntington, Samuel P. *The Common Defense*. New York: Columbia University Press, 1961.

Kaufmann, William. *The McNamara Strategy*. New York: Harper and Row, 1964.

Schilling, Warner R., Paul Y. Hammond, and Glen H. Snyder. *Strategy, Politics, and Defense Budgets*. New York: Columbia University Press, 1962.

CHAPTER FIVE

Soviet Military Strategy

Throughout the postwar period the United States has viewed the Soviet Union as its chief military opponent. The main thrust of American policy has been toward the deterrence of military actions by the Soviet Union or her allies. More recently attention has focused on Communist China as a separate enemy of the United States, whose actions—as is now recognized—are not necessarily in coordination with, and are certainly not controlled by, the Soviet Union. This chapter will discuss Soviet military doctrine, particularly as it relates to Soviet strategy in dealing with the American strategic nuclear threat and with Europe.

Before turning to the substance of Soviet military doctrine, it may be useful to consider briefly the nature of our sources of information about Soviet and Chinese military doctrine. Statements issued by the two governments are one such source. The amount of literature from the Soviet Union is much greater than that from Communist China; but both countries release statements of general foreign policy and, in the case of the Soviet Union, statements on military issues. The Soviets have released some books dealing specifically with military strategy, the most important of which was edited by Soviet General Sokolovsky and was entitled *Military Strategy*. This book, which purports to be a comprehensive statement of Soviet doctrine, has been widely analyzed in the West as a source of insight into Soviet military strategy. In the last several years much material on Sino-Soviet military relations and the military strategy of the two countries has been revealed in the polemics of the Sino-Soviet dispute.

A second major source of data—one perhaps too little exploited—is the actions of the two countries. We should be able to learn much more about Sino-Soviet military doctrine from actions in Korea, in Berlin, and in Cuba than from articles in military journals.

Finally, the military-budget decisions of the two countries can be examined. Both countries publish a single one-line item on defense in their annual budget but obviously spend a good deal more on defense. There has been much work done on the size and form of the Soviet defense budgets, some of it released by the Joint Economic Committee of Congress. Other material on the output of the two countries' defense budgets is available in the Institute for Strategic Studies' annual pamphlet, the *Military Balance*; in the American defense-budget hearings; and in such American publications as *Aviation Week*. Studies published by such organizations as the RAND Corporation are also available; authors of such publications have access to classified data.

Though our understanding of Soviet and Chinese military doctrine is necessarily more limited than our understanding of American doctrine, we now have a working knowledge of Soviet policy, at least for the early years of the postwar period. We can even say a great deal with some confidence about their current doctrine.

SOVIET GENERAL WAR STRATEGY

The primary concern of the Soviet Union's military policy during the entire postwar period has been the deterrence of an American nuclear attack, so that the Soviets would be free to pursue their objectives by other means without fearing an American attack. In the period until the mid-1950's, the Soviet Union was completely dependent for deterrence of an American attack on threats to retaliate against American allies rather than against the United States, since the Soviets had no significant capability to attack the American homeland. During this early period the major Soviet military deterrent was a large ground force capable of seizing and holding Western Europe. In addition to its large ground army, the Soviet Union placed great emphasis on air defense. The Soviets have continued up to the present time to spend a much greater percentage of their defense budget on active defense than the United States does. While the United States, for example, has viewed the decision to proceed with a ballistic-missile defense as a difficult and complicated one, the Soviets have acted as though it were obvious that both sides would develop ballistic-missile-defense capabilities, given the importance of being able to defend oneself against an attack. As has already been noted, the Soviet active defense force is much larger than that of the United States; but also, because of its emphasis on a day, good-weather capability, Soviet active defenses are not particularly effective against the night or bad-weather attack, which the United States is capable of mounting. Both the size and shape of the force seem to have been guided and influenced by bureaucratic tendencies as much as, or perhaps more than, a positive strategic doctrine. The doctrine, insofar as it existed, apparently aimed at using active defense and passive civil defense in order to reduce the damage that the United States could do to the Soviet Union.

At the same time, immediately following the Second World War, the Soviet Union engaged in a crash program for the development of atomic weapons. The existence of the program demonstrates the danger of relying on writings from the Soviet Union, which, until after the death of Stalin, claimed no interest in atomic warfare. Rather, it was suggested that Stalin believed that "permanent operating factors" emphasizing the social and economic structure of the countries would determine the outcome of a war. In fact, decision makers in the Soviet Union recognized the great importance of atomic weapons and the effect they would have on warfare and on diplomacy. In the postwar period the Soviet Union developed atomic weapons very quickly and hydrogen bombs even more quickly, perhaps even before the United States. At the same time the Soviets launched a crash research and development program on delivery systems, including long-range bombers and intercontinental ballistic missiles.

The final part of the Soviet plan for deterrence was the adoption of a relatively moderate foreign policy designed to deter politically American over-reaction. The Soviets recognized that they were in a state of military weakness and, consequently, could not afford to press too far in attempting to expand the area under Communist control.

Soviet Intercontinental Capability

In the middle 1950's the Soviet Union began to develop some capability for attacking, with a small strategic bomber force, the United States. However, its strategic nuclear force was still substantially limited. The Soviet Union decided not to produce anywhere near as many strategic delivery vehicles—both bombers in the 1950's and ICBM's in the late 1950's and early 1960's—as they could have. For both, Western analysts had predicted a much larger Soviet force. To the question, why did the Soviet Union choose to build only a small number of bombers and missiles, several answers have been suggested.

The first explanation is that the Soviets simply believed that a very small force was sufficient for deterrence purposes. Western eyes tended to contrast the small force with the much larger American capability against the Soviet Union. Nevertheless, to the Soviets, their capabilities represented perceptible increases over their previous forces. Moreover, even in the late 1950's the Soviets apparently were unaware of the ramifications of the vulnerability of a strategic force to an attack on the ground; they probably believed that their force was more effective than it actually was. In terms of political advantage, however, the Soviets were certainly correct if they believed that they would get perceptible deterrence from a very small force that could reach the United States.

Secondly, the Soviets were operating within a much tighter economic and financial constraint than the American government was. The Soviet GNP was significantly smaller, and the Soviets had a greater urge to spend money on stimulating the growth of heavy industry. In addition, as was mentioned earlier, the Soviets devoted very large percentages of their resources to air defense and continued to maintain very large ground forces.

Thirdly, the Soviets apparently thought they could bluff the West into believing they had a much larger strategic force than they actually had. The American government credited the Soviets with having a much greater capability—both bombers and missiles—and certainly in the case of the missiles there was a deliberate attempt on the part of Khrushchev to deceive the West. The Soviets presumably felt that a very small force coupled with exaggerated statements could have almost as great, or perhaps as great, a political payoff as a much larger force.

Finally, in the case of ICBM's, the Soviets must have recognized the great limitations of their first-generation strategic vehicles. Their missiles were large, clumsy, slow, expensive to construct and maintain, and difficult to protect. Thus, the Soviets may have decided to wait until they had a second-generation missile more closely resembling the American Minuteman, before proceeding into large-scale production. If that is true, the 1960's may see the Soviet Union producing a large strategic force, perhaps of five hundred or more strategic delivery vehicles.

Current Strategic Doctrine

During the past several years, Soviet statements and actions have revealed that Soviet thinking about strategic questions closely parallels Western thought. The Soviets now accept the critical importance of surprise and of the first strike in the early hours of a general nuclear war. They acknowledge also that the early stages of a war can be decisive, although they continue to discuss the phase of large-scale ground fighting that follows a strategic exchange (and seem to assume that they could invade and capture Western Europe). The most important items in their budget and in their policy statements relate to warfare in the early hours and the strategic nuclear exchange.

The Soviets are now aware of the importance of developing strategic forces that are relatively invulnerable to a first strike. Their second-generation missiles appear to be smaller and better protected than the first-generation missiles; the Soviets are also building up a submarine-launched missile capability. They have always put great stress on the importance of command and control—for internal political reasons, tied up with their desire to insure that the Soviet Army could never successfully challenge the Communist party, as well as for strategic reasons.

At least in their public statements the Soviets reject any possibility of limiting a general nuclear war. Their verbal reaction to the McNamara controlled-response doctrine (discussed in Chapter

Seven) suggested that this doctrine was an attempt by the United States to legitimatize a first strike against the Soviet Union. The Soviets denied that it was possible to limit a nuclear war and stated that they would attack American cities in the event of an ✓ American strategic attack on the Soviet Union. However, the private Soviet reaction to the notion of limiting general nuclear war may be very different or at least in a state of flux. Once the Soviets are confident of their own ability of surviving a strategic attack, they may be willing to discuss publicly the possibility of war limitation.

In late 1957 the Soviets began to talk about the great destruction that would result on both sides from a general nuclear war. Khrushchev publicly rejected what was identified as the Marxist-Leninist notion of the inevitability of war and suggested instead that war could be avoided because there were reasonable men on both sides and that war had to be avoided because of the great destruction it would bring. The Soviets stressed the deterrence that would result from their threat to destroy cities with multi-megaton weapons. In their polemics with the Chinese on the question of nuclear war, they accused the Chinese of not sufficiently understanding the destructive power of nuclear weapons. They pointed out that nuclear weapons do not observe class distinctions.

In the early 1960's the arms race between the United States and the Soviet Union entered a new phase, one in which the Soviet Union, for the first time, had the option of matching American strategic capability. For this reason, the interaction between the two sides is now much more important in shaping decisions, at least in the United States. The United States recognizes that what it can do, the Soviets can do; therefore, there may be some value in mutual restraint. The Soviets seem to be less aware of the strong interaction of the two strategic postures and do not appear to be planning to match quantitatively American capability. Qualitatively, they are now slowly doing so; the Soviets should have a significant number, perhaps hundreds, of well-protected strategic forces sometime in the late 1960's or early 1970's. The capability of the force will perhaps be as good as that of the United States, at least in terms of accuracy and reliability, if not in reaction time or hardness.

The Soviets appear to be surpassing the United States in two fields. The first of these is ballistic-missile defense. The United States may be ahead of the Soviet Union in terms of research and development, but the Soviets may have begun deployment first. The Soviet Union is also exceeding the United States in the development of very large weapons. The Soviet Union has tested a weapon approaching one hundred megatons of power, perhaps two to three times greater than any weapon tested by the United States. The Soviets have developed such weapons for large-scale city destruction.

Whether the Soviets are trying to match the United States in the size of their strategic force has not been established. However, the evidence suggests that they probably will be content with a force significantly smaller than the American intercontinental capability. As has already been mentioned, budget constraints are such that the Soviets may feel that they must make do with a small force. In addition, the United States has a perceptible lead in absolute numbers and has demonstrated that it can, and intends to, stay very far ahead. Finally, and perhaps most critical, there must be considerable doubt in the Soviet Union as to the military need for a force as large as that of the United States, even if the Soviets accept the possibility or desirability of a counterforce no-cities war.

Moreover, by their threat to Europe, the Soviets will probably continue to try to deter the United States. This threat now consists of not only a ground force equipped with tactical nuclear weapons but also approximately one thousand IRBM's and MRBM's and a medium-range bomber force. Europe still very much remains a hostage to deter the United States.

SOVIET STRATEGY FOR EUROPE

One key element of Soviet strategy for Europe has already been discussed; that is, the notion that Western Europe can be used to deter the United States from attacking the Soviet Union.

The most blatant use of Soviet military power in the postwar period has occurred in Eastern Europe. In the early postwar period the Soviet Army seized control in these areas and put into power Communist governments that were then totally subservient to the Soviet Union. The continued presence of the Soviet Army in Central Europe has discouraged countries from leaving the Soviet bloc; and, of course, the forces were actually used in East Germany and in Hungary to suppress efforts to change the governments in power.

The Soviet Union apparently never even contemplated the overt use of military force west of the Iron Curtain. Evidence now available suggests that the Soviet Union did not consider the march to the English Channel, the threat upon which NATO has concentrated. The Soviet fear of atomic retaliation by the United States was always present, as well as recognition of the problems that would ensue in trying to bring Western Europe under Stalinist control. Finally, the Soviets have probably been aware of the unreliability of the satellite armies and populations and hence the vulnerability of their supply lines. However, even if the Soviets never contemplated a march to the channel, the relative military balance in Central Europe has influenced the political evolution of countries on both sides of the Iron Curtain.

The Soviet posture vis-à-vis Western Europe has been, and continues to be, a defensive and deterrent one. The positioning of Soviet ground forces in Eastern Europe and the very limited logistics capability of these forces suggests an orientation primarily aimed at defending against a Western attack. Perhaps for this reason, the Soviet Army has produced in quantity fighters and surface-to-air missiles. The size of the Soviet Army in Europe has been a matter of some confusion in Western analyses. In the early postwar period the Soviets were credited with 175 divisions, a number that remained constant despite reorganizations of the Soviet Army and reductions in the number of ground troops. More recently, estimates by the United States have been less than half that number; and it appears that the Soviet Union does not have now, if it ever had, overwhelming conventional superiority on the central front in Europe.

The Soviets apparently have been no more successful than the West in developing a coherent doctrine for the employment of tactical nuclear weapons. Soviet forces are capable of fighting both conventionally and with tactical nuclear weapons; however, the Soviet tactical nuclear arsenal is much smaller and much less sophisticated than that of the United States. Not until the mid-

1960's did the Soviets begin to introduce somewhat smaller tactical nuclear weapons into the operating arsenals of their ground troops. The Soviets presumably believe that if nuclear weapons were used, it would be over a large area and with relatively large warheads. Whatever their own views are on tactical nuclear war, the Soviets, for internal political reasons, may fear the dispersal of tactical nuclear weapons among their ground troops.

The major Soviet use of military force in Western Europe has been as a threat in order to accomplish specific political purposes. Much of this effort has centered on Berlin. The Soviets have attempted to use their conventional superiority in the local area to force the West out of the city or at least into accepting East German sovereignty over the access routes to Berlin. The Soviets have warned those nations that have permitted American nuclear weapons to be stationed in their territory that they have left themselves open to the danger of Soviet nuclear attack. The most specific Soviet threats ensued in 1960, when the Soviets shot down an American U-2. The Soviets warned that they would destroy with a missile any base from which an American U-2 took off or landed while engaged in overflying the Soviet Union.

The basic Soviet aims in Europe have been to consolidate their control over Eastern Europe; to try to gain control over, or at least neutralize, Germany; and to drive the United States from Europe. They have used a combination of military pressure and various political tactics, including peace offensives, in order to accomplish these objectives. The importance attached to different objectives has varied through the postwar period; but, in all cases, the Soviet military power has served as an important backdrop.

THE THIRD WORLD

As has already been stated, Soviet military strategy has focused on Western Europe and strategic deterrence of the United States. The Soviets have been much less interested in the third world; however, they have been concerned with two problems in this area. The first is wars of national liberation; the second, their alliance with China.

The Soviets continue to support wars of national liberation, at least in principle, and have in fact been willing to aid some revolutionary wars, such as the war in Vietnam. This subject will be discussed in more detail in Chapter Twelve.

The Soviets entered into a treaty of alliance with Communist China in 1950. This treaty commits the Soviet Union to come to the aid of China in the event of an attack by Japan or an ally of Japan. From time to time during crises, the Soviets have reiterated their support for China; they seem prepared to intervene in case the existence of the Communist regime in China is threatened. To what extent the Russians would intervene in the event of a lesser attack on China remains uncertain; for, it may be that the Russians have been giving some thought in the last two or three years to another problem: deterring the Chinese along the Sino-Soviet border.

SELECTED BIBLIOGRAPHY

Dinerstein, Herbert S., Leon Gouré, and Thomas W. Wolfe, eds. *Soviet Military Strategy*. Englewood Cliffs, N.J.: Prentice-Hall, 1963.

Dinerstein, Herbert S. *War and the Soviet Union*. New York: Frederick A. Praeger, 1959.

Horelick, Arnold, and Myron Rush. *Strategic Power and Soviet Foreign Policy*. Chicago: University of Chicago Press, 1966.

Mackintosh, Malcolm. *Strategy and Tactics of Soviet Foreign Policy*. London: Oxford University Press, 1962.

Wolfe, Thomas W. *Soviet Strategy at the Crossroads*. Cambridge, Mass.: Harvard University Press, 1964.

CHAPTER SIX

Chinese Military Strategy

With the growing belief in the unwillingness of the Soviet Union to use its military force and with the growth of Chinese military power, particularly nuclear power, the People's Republic of China has received more attention from military strategists and defense planners. One manifestation of this development, accelerated by the Sino-Soviet split and the war in Vietnam, was the consideration given by the United States to the installation of a ballistic-missile defense directed against China. Because much less has been written about China, we will attempt in this chapter to consider Chinese military strategy in the context of Chinese foreign policy.

Chinese foreign-policy objectives have been, and continue to be, subordinated to domestic objectives: the preservation of the regime and the economic growth and industrialization of the society. Defense budgets have been modest, certainly in contrast to the generally held image of a very militant and military China, and even by universal standards of expenditures on defense. The defense spending appears to be defensively oriented—that is, oriented largely towards the objective of defending Chinese territory —against a Chinese Nationalist invasion or perhaps an American invasion, rather than toward offensive operations that would require, for example, strong air power.

In addition, the Chinese have concentrated on averting a clash with the United States. Chinese Communist strategy during the Chinese civil war was influenced by the problem of avoiding United States' entry into the war and of ending the war without provoking an American attack. Despite the very great importance the Chinese have attached to capturing Taiwan and eliminating the regime there, they have not engaged in any activities which could have brought them into a direct military clash with the United States. Since June of 1950, when the United States committed itself to the defense of Taiwan, there has not been any Chinese Communist attempt to take Taiwan. The only actions have been against the offshore islands of Quemoy and Matsu, and these attacks have been very cautiously maneuvered. In Indochina and India as well, whatever the Chinese motivations may have been, the restraints on their actions have obviously been influenced by fear of provoking an American attack.

Turning more specifically to foreign-policy objectives of the Peking regime, we can identify some that are peculiarly "Chinese." The urgency involved in their attainment, or the way in which Peking seeks to attain them, clearly is influenced by the fact that the Peking regime is a Communist regime; but these objectives are ones that any strong Chinese government would have. There are other objectives that a non-Communist Chinese government would not have and that are equally important to Chinese policy.

The most important national-interest objective is the recovery of lost territories—territories that are part of China or that the country's leaders see as being part of China and, consequently, try to regain for the regime. The major action for this objective has been the conquest of Tibet (which the Chinese Nationalists supported). The current outstanding irredenta is, of course, Taiwan; and the conquest of this territory has been a primary foreign-policy objective since 1949.

Closely related to the incorporation of Taiwan into the Peking regime is the elimination of the rival regime on Taiwan, which claims to be the government of all of China. The Chinese have adopted a policy of not recognizing, or entering into diplomatic relations with, any country that has relations with the Taiwan regime.

Finally, the establishment of Chinese dominance in Asia is an important Chinese Communist objective, although it receives less attention than the others mentioned so far. It is one that would be pursued by any strong government that controlled the mainland of China.

Turning to specific Communist interests, the Peking regime wishes to increase the area under Communist control as distinguished from the area under Chinese control. This has led in part to their willingness to support Communist regimes—now, in particular, those Communist regimes that, according to the Chinese, take the correct Marxist-Leninist line. Albania is a good example. The Chinese have been giving this country both substantial foreign aid, given Chinese capability, and vigorous diplomatic support. The Chinese now attach great importance to having the international Communist movement pursue what the Chinese consider to be the correct line rather than a modern-revisionist line, notably in determining the best way to expand the area under Communist control and to bring about the overthrow of imperialism and then of capitalist and non-Communist regimes. It is very difficult to maintain that the Chinese did not give, for their own sake, high priority to the establishment of Communist regimes in Africa, Latin America, and the Middle East. The Chinese cannot really hope to make major gains in terms of purely Chinese interest from the establishment of Communist regimes in these areas, yet the evidence from the Sino-Soviet dispute suggests that they are willing to have the international Communist movement pursue the "correct" line at the expense of deterioration of their relations with the Soviets.

THE CURRENT WORLD SITUATION

The Chinese attach great weight to a correct appraisal of the world situation: they maintain that the first step in deciding what to do is to determine the nature of the current historical period— the details of the world situation in relation to particular countries and their problems. Therefore, getting some feeling for the Chinese appraisal of the current world situation is important because it provides an important key to understanding Chinese foreign policy.

The Chinese view the attempt by the Soviet Union and the United States to establish hegemony in the world as the central characteristic of the current period. This attempt is called a *détente* in the West and "peaceful co-existence" by the Russians, but the Chinese see nothing good about it. Rather, they see it as an endeavor to dominate the world: to separate the world into two spheres of influence and to prevent other countries from attaining the power, particularly nuclear power, necessary to maintain their own place in the world. Obviously, for the Chinese, this is a situation that must be vigorously opposed. It hinders China because it means that China is not likely to capture Taiwan very soon nor to get nuclear weapons. The Chinese also feel it is dangerous for the international Communist movement. If, as the Chinese believe, the Russians have abandoned Marxist-Leninism for a modern-revisionist line (referred to by the Chinese as "goulash communism"), then the Russians can no longer be interested in the revolution and significantly endanger the future of international communism.

The emergence of an intermediate group of nations that opposes this trend towards a Soviet-American monopoly and that can in the long run defeat this attempt has been for the Chinese an encouraging, new development in the world situation. The countries in this group are China and France; but the Chinese hope that more countries in Europe and other areas of the world will join this intermediate zone. Peking undoubtedly hopes Tokyo will play a major role in opposing Soviet-American hegemony. By being anti-status quo and by being fundamentally opposed to a world controlled by two superpowers, these intermediate countries, partly by their own actions and partly by getting support from smaller countries, can prevent the establishment of this kind of dominance.

In the last few years the Chinese have seen a much greater variety of conditions in the underdeveloped nations than they did previously. Three categories for underdeveloped nations may be distinguished: revolutionary situations, particularly in countries still under imperialist control (in the southern part of Africa, for example); countries which have stable, friendly regimes (governments with which they feel they can work—countries on their own periphery or revolutionary regimes in other parts of the

); and small nations that are allied to the United States or
vise have an anti-Chinese posture. Chinese optimism about
the third world culminated in early 1965, when the Chinese had
great hopes for the proposed Afro-Asian conference. Since then
they have had to recognize their limited ability to influence countries, even revolutionary regimes far from their borders.

In contrast to Chinese sentiment about Soviet communism—
that the international Communist movement has been significantly
endangered by the revisionist regime in the Soviet Union—the
Chinese do feel very positively that the permanence of the Chinese Communist regime has been assured. In the last several years
the Chinese have recovered from the very severe domestic crises
which they experienced in 1960 and 1961. They survived both
very serious crop failures, largely based on natural causes combined with the disaster of the commune attempt, and the with-
drawal of Soviet technicians, which produced a crisis in industry,
at a time when China was more isolated than it is now. Having
survived the crises in 1960 and 1961, China gained a great deal
more confidence: if the regime could survive that, in effect, it
could survive anything.

Evidently the Chinese were somewhat surprised and pleased at
the relative ease with which they did come through their difficult
period; in particular, they may have been surprised by the fact
that the United States did not exploit this period of weakness. In
1962, for example, the Chinese feared that the United States
might support a landing by the Chinese Nationalists on the mainland and that this might lead to large-scale uprisings. The failure
of the United States to exploit this situation and the fact—which
the Chinese report—that the United States in the Warsaw talks
gave guarantees that it would not help the Chinese Nationalists
to land on the mainland, have led the Chinese to reevaluate the
real threat posed by the Nationalists. The Chinese now feel that
neither the Chinese Nationalists nor internal elements in China
present any serious threat to the maintenance of the Communist
regime.

The fact that the Chinese have let the Sino-Soviet rift go as far
as it has, is a manifestation of Chinese confidence. If the Chinese
still feared—as they did in the early days of the regime—the possibility of an American attack aimed at destroying the Communist

regime, they would not have let the dispute go so far. They would have paid whatever price was necessary to keep the rift from becoming the bitter public dispute that it has become; they would have felt the need for Soviet support.

In the long run, the Chinese are confident that their own objectives and the objectives of the international Communist movement will be obtained.

THE ROLE OF FORCE

Turning more specifically to strategic issues, we may begin by asking: How do the Chinese feel force can, and should, be used? Mao has said that power comes from the barrel of a gun and that politics should control the gun. For the Peking regime, force is a legitimate instrument of both internal and external policy; it must be put at all times under political control and must be used in limited, controlled ways in the pursuit of particular foreign-policy objectives. The Chinese see nothing wrong with using force for political purposes, and they have demonstrated their willingness to use force for a variety of specific objectives.

The fundamental principle of Maoist military doctrine is the notion of going from a very weak position to a strong position in which a country's objectives can be realized. Maoism holds that with a very small force a country can triumph ultimately against overwhelming odds by gradually increasing its strength while diminishing the strength of its opponent. The Chinese used this strategy in the civil war and are now trying to follow it in their foreign policy.

The statement that a country should strategically despise its enemy but tactically respect him—a doctrine which the Chinese specifically apply to the United States—simply means that in the long run a country can defeat its enemy by using the proper tactics but in the short run must recognize that the enemy is stronger and, therefore, must be respected. It is in this light that we should examine such statements as "The United States is a paper tiger." It means that in the long run the United States can be defeated by proper strategy; it does not mean that nuclear weapons cannot destroy China, if the United States chooses to use them now. In the same way we must view the statement that man will triumph over weapons. It does not mean that if a nuclear weapon and a man are in the same place, the nuclear weapon cannot explode and kill the man; it means that in the long run what will determine the political orientation of countries is the views of men and not the nature of the weapons system. This was true in China; this the Chinese believe is true in Indochina; and they believe ultimately that it will be true everywhere. The system of communism can spread by gaining the allegiance of men regardless of who controls what weapons in the short run.

Nuclear War

There is a widespread view that the Chinese do not understand nuclear war; do not fear nuclear war; and, in fact, even desire nuclear war; and that they lack an understanding of the realities of the Nuclear Age. This is, however, a completely false picture of the Chinese. It is a picture that has been spread largely by the Soviet Union, because it happens to fulfill a Soviet objective: to convince the West that the Soviet Union wants a *détente* because it has lunatics on its border. However, if one looks at what the Chinese say and what they have done in various crisis situations, their point of view becomes clear: that nuclear war would, in fact, be a great disaster for the world and, in particular, for China and the Communist regime. They are under no illusion that the leaders of Communist China, as well as the industrialization of China which the leaders have directed, would be spared, even in a rather small nuclear war.

They probably believe that communism, not capitalism, would survive as the world system of government and that China and Russia would survive as political entities. In addition, the Chinese have contended, especially with the Russians, that to emphasize the destructiveness of nuclear war and to make speeches as Khrushchev had been doing, and now President Johnson has been doing, about how many people would be killed in how many minutes in a nuclear war, is politically self-defeating. It opens up a country to political blackmail by its opponent with nuclear weapons; it demoralizes a country and is exceptionally dangerous when that country does not have nuclear weapons. It is unreasonable to expect the Chinese to stress the dangers of nuclear war when they do not have nuclear weapons and are facing in the

Far East an opponent who does. The Chinese have sought to capitalize on the misconception that they do not fear nuclear war. In the early 1960's they were tending in this direction; and the standard line of Western analysts was to say that while the Chinese assert that they do not fear nuclear war, in fact, they really do. Nor is it very clear that the Chinese are not asserting that nuclear war would be good for China. This is partly a recognition on their part that to play the role of lunatic can be in some situations a source of strength, if their opponents are convinced that the Chinese are not afraid of their opponents' weapons. However, it can also be a source of weakness in the sense that China's enemies might be more intent on trying to destroy the Peking regime if they thought that the Chinese were lunatics.

There has been, we are told, a major revision in the Soviet outlook on war; the Soviets now believe that nuclear war is no longer fatally inevitable. This is not as great a change as it is sometimes made out to be; but, whatever kind of change it is, the Chinese have also accepted it. The Chinese believe that war is inevitable—wars of national revolution or wars between capitalist societies—but that nuclear war between the Communist bloc and the capitalist bloc is not inevitable.

The Chinese do differ from the Russians on the issue of how to prevent nuclear war. The Chinese argue that if a country wants peace, it must prepare for war: that the way to prevent nuclear war with the West is to build up both the military strength and the will and determination of the Communist bloc. Several implications are intended: The Soviets should strive for superiority over the United States in nuclear forces and should not accept inferiority; the Soviets should help the Chinese to become a nuclear power, because the more nuclear powers there are in the Communist bloc, the easier it is to deter the United States; the Soviet Union should not emphasize its fear of nuclear war, the danger of nuclear war, nor the importance of *détente* or disarmament. The Chinese argue that disarmament is not attainable as long as there are capitalist countries; therefore, by concerning itself with disarmament, a country exposes its fear of nuclear war. As a result, nuclear war becomes more, rather than less, likely; the leadership of a country is encouraged to push the controlling button if it believes that its opponent does not fear nuclear war.

Closely related to Chinese concepts of nuclear war is the Chinese image of the role of the strategic balance in international politics. From the image often held—that to the Chinese, men are more important than weapons and that nuclear weapons do not really count—it might be surmised that the Chinese attach little importance to the strategic balance; in fact, the reverse is true. The Chinese have placed more emphasis on the nuclear balance than either the United States or the Soviet Union. They have attempted to some extent to measure historical periods by the nature of the nuclear balance. The famous Chinese assertion in 1957, that the East Wind was now prevailing over the West Wind, is a reflection both of the importance the Chinese attach to the nuclear balance and their belief that historical periods and historical possibilities change when the nuclear balance changes. The Chinese believed that a major change would occur in 1957 for two reasons: they thought the Russians were becoming stronger than the Americans and that Russia was about to give them their own nuclear capability. By 1960 they realized that neither of these two predictions would, in fact, materialize. This realization, plus China's increasing isolation from Russia, has resulted in a much more vigorous pursuit of an independent Chinese nuclear capability.

The fundamental Chinese motivation for acquiring a nuclear capability is based on the following reasoning: all great powers have nuclear weapons; China is a great power; therefore, China must have nuclear weapons. In this sense, the Chinese desire for nuclear weapons goes back to 1946, when the Chinese saw that atomic weapons would be an important component of power and decided that in the long run China would have to become an atomic power. The desire for nuclear weapons is a basic drive of the regime—one that is unlikely to be affected by the details of technology or the cost involved.

A second, more concrete objective for having nuclear weapons is to deter an American attack on China—particularly one growing out of a crisis or military encounter in the Far East. Chinese policy will be aimed, at least over the next decade, at deterring the United States by threatening Asian cities rather than directly threatening the United States. By holding Asia hostage against an American nuclear attack, the Chinese will pursue a policy similar to that implemented by the Russians in Europe.

Nuclear weapons are important to the Chinese as a means of increasing their power within the Communist world. The Chinese feel that if they are ever going to challenge successfully the current regime in Moscow, they will have to do it on a basis of increased power, namely, nuclear power. Finally, they see nuclear weapons as being of some marginal value in support of their political objectives in Asia—as a threat against Asian countries.

Conventional War

When we examine the role of conventional forces as an instrument of Chinese foreign policy, we see most strikingly that the Chinese have a very strong desire to avoid major conventional war, primarily for two reasons: the economic cost involved in preparing for a major conventional war—the amount of equipment and training that would be necessary—and the economic cost of participating in the war, both in terms of resources used and in terms of possible destruction. In addition, probably as important, is the realization that any large-scale deployment of conventional forces runs the danger of provoking an American attack. The Chinese have been willing to use very limited kinds of military force for very specific purposes in the Taiwan Straits and on the Sino-Indian border.

The Chinese have used major force in only two kinds of situations: first, when they felt there was no danger of intervention by an outside power, for example, in Tibet, where they thought that the territory they were attacking was part of China and consequently committed what is the clearest case of overt aggression in the postwar period; secondly, when they felt the alternative of not using major military force was more dangerous than engaging in this kind of encounter, as in Korea.

In conclusion, what can be said about the Chinese long-run view of their own, and the world, situation? Most important to them is the establishment of China as a major world, and nuclear, power. The Chinese believe that they have successfully survived the internal crises of the early sixties and are on their way—be it a long way—toward economic development and industrialization.

Peking also envisions the establishment of Chinese hegemony in Asia, the elimination of American bases, and the recognition by all Asian countries of China's dominance. Furthermore, they see the destruction of the Republic of China and the incorporation of

Taiwan into the Peking regime, although they have no clear notion of how this is going to come about. They accept the fact that the United States will continue to be their major enemy and that there is no possibility of any settlement with the United States. To seek a *détente* would be dangerous and meaningless; they simply have to resign themselves to the fact that for the indefinite future they face a very powerful enemy in the United States.

In terms of relations with other countries—the Soviet Union, Western Europe, the underdeveloped areas—Peking's views are probably not very clearly defined. They hope that the current Soviet regime will be replaced by a true Marxist-Leninist regime, which will realign with China; that they can establish friendly relations with West European countries, in order to make credit and trade agreements; and that in Africa and Latin America the number of revolutionary regimes will increase. They probably are not very optimistic about any of these occurring—to the extent that they want them to—in the next ten or fifteen years.

China will remain, then, a tough, calculating, anti-status-quo power, with a good appreciation of what goes on in the world and a good understanding of the objectives and policies of the United States and of other countries. With growing power—and ultimately nuclear power—China will pose an increasing threat to Western and Russian interests in the foreseeable future.

SELECTED BIBLIOGRAPHY

Halperin, Morton H. *China and the Bomb*. New York: Frederick A. Praeger, 1965.
Halperin, Morton H., and Dwight H. Perkins. *Communist China and Arms Control*. New York: Frederick A. Praeger, 1965.
Hinton, Harold. *Communist China in World Politics*. Boston: Houghton Mifflin Co., 1966.
Hsieh, Alice. *Communist China's Strategy in the Nuclear Age*. Englewood Cliffs, N.J.: Prentice-Hall, 1962.
Whiting, Allen. *China Crosses the Yalu*. New York: The Macmillan Co., 1960.

CHAPTER SEVEN

General War: The Strategy of Controlled Response

Many popular discussions of general nuclear war, as well as the accepted view of the American government—at least until the early 1960's—have assumed that any general nuclear war would be uncontrolled and uncontrollable. Strategic nuclear forces have been seen as necessary to deter a nuclear war, but what happens after a war has begun has not been considered. Without denying that any general nuclear war would be unprecedented distaster and that it would be extremely difficult to control the use of nuclear weapons once it began, the American government has sought to develop a strategy that would at least allow for the possibility of control and of limiting damage to the United States, if a general nuclear war were to begin.

Planning and procurement for controlling a general nuclear war began soon after Robert S. McNamara assumed the office of Secretary of Defense in 1961; however, the first public statement of the controlled-response strategy was made by the Secretary in a speech at Ann Arbor, Michigan in June, 1962. At that time, repeating—according to a number of press reports—what he had told the NATO Council in December of the previous year, Mr. McNamara declared:

> The United States has come to the conclusion that to the extent feasible, basic military strategy in a possible general nuclear war

should be approached in much the same way that more conventional military operations have been regarded in the past. That is to say, principal military objectives, in the event of a nuclear war stemming from a major attack on the Alliance, should be the destruction of the enemy's military forces, not of its civilian population.

The very strength and nature of the Alliance forces make it possible for us to retain, even in the face of a massive surprise attack, sufficient reserve striking power to destroy an enemy society if driven to it. In other words, we are giving a possible opponent the strongest imaginable incentive to refrain from striking our own cities.

More important than the specific strategy being espoused by the Secretary of Defense at that time, was the basic, underlying attitude toward general nuclear war. Mr. McNamara was denying that general nuclear war was inevitable and that it necessarily had to be an orgy of city destruction. He asserted that the United States would strive to keep its own military forces under control —not only up to, but during, any general nuclear war. Further, in discussing the incentives for the Soviet Union, the speech extended the notion of deterrence and bargaining into the period after the inception of a general nuclear war. The speech negated that deterrence could only work before war and that both sides would simply employ all of their capability in order to destroy as much of their enemy's military force and civilian population as possible.

Going beyond these general attitudes, which have continued to shape American general war strategy, Mr. McNamara announced specifically that the United States had removed Soviet cities from its first priority target list. He declared that the United States would not strike Soviet cities unless the Soviets attacked American cities first. He noted that there was no good military reason for striking cities and that the effort of the United States would be to destroy Soviet strategic forces in order to limit whatever damage they could do to the United States and possibly to enable the United States to win the war. Far from suggesting that such a strategy could make nuclear war clean and relatively humane, the speech indicated the Administration's beliefs that no matter how a nuclear war was conducted, the destruction would be very great, and that there was simply no guarantee that the war would end without city destruction. Nevertheless, the United States would do all that it could to avoid attacks on cities in the United States, the Soviet Union, or in Western Europe, and would hold some of its forces—presumably its Polaris missiles—in reserve, to attack Soviet cities should that become necessary.

Though the particular emphasis given by Mr. McNamara has been somewhat altered over the succeeding years, the basic strategy of controlled response has become a firm part of American strategic doctrine. Therefore, we will briefly examine the origins of controlled response before considering the changes in emphasis which have occurred since 1962.

ORIGINS OF THE CONTROLLED-RESPONSE STRATEGY

It is possible to identify intellectual, technological, and political factors that contributed to the enunciation of a controlled-response doctrine by the United States in the early 1960's.

The McNamara team came into the Pentagon at a time when the United States already had a large bomber force and had committed itself to producing a very substantial number of missiles, partly on the assumption that the Soviet Union would create a very large intercontinental-missile force. The new Kennedy Administration felt the need for developing a rationale for the use of existing weapons systems. Thus in this case (as well as in others), to some extent doctrine followed the development of weapons systems. The Administration asked itself what could be done with the Minuteman and Polaris forces that were to be produced within the next several years. For reasons to be indicated below, this force particularly lent itself to a doctrine of control and of limited response.

In the mid-1950's many strategic analysts who dealt with the problems of limited war had confined themselves mainly to analysis of *local-war* situations. By 1960 it had become apparent that there was no sharp break between attacks on Soviet and American territory and other kinds of wars, and that an attack on the homelands of the superpowers need not automatically trigger all-out war. Thus, concern for limited war was extended to strategic nuclear war. As a result, interest in control, bargaining, and communication during general wars was aroused.

At the same time an interest in the subject of "arms control" developed. Analysts began to take seriously the role that negotiated or more tacit agreements could have in limiting or directing the arms race. This thinking quite naturally was applied to strategic nuclear systems, as well as other kinds of weapons; control and political use of strategic forces, and bargaining and communication, even during a war, also became important possibilities.

Thus, the continuing search for a doctrine to exploit existing weapons systems, the extension of previous limited-war thought, and the growth of arms-control thinking combined to lay the intellectual foundations for a strategy of controlled response.

At the same time, technology was changing in ways which made controlled response seem both necessary and feasible. During the course of the 1950's, the destructive power available to the United States and the Soviet Union increased tremendously. In the beginning of the decade, both countries developed thermonuclear weapons with much greater destructive power than the earlier atomic bombs had had. At the same time, the arsenals of the two countries increased very greatly; and the Soviets attained for the first time an ability to inflict substantial damage on the United States. By the end of the decade it was clear that any war in which the two superpowers sought to inflict maximum damage on each other would lead to the virtual destruction of the two societies. This enormous destructive power by itself generated pressures, not only to prevent a nuclear war, but also to see if there were not things that could be done in peacetime which might serve to limit damage, should war occur.

If weapons were becoming more destructive, they were also becoming easier to control; the destructive power of some individual weapons was even reduced. The major change in the American strategic force programmed for the early 1960's was the rapid introduction of a large number of Polaris and Minuteman missiles superimposed on, but to some extent replacing, early generation Atlas and Titan missiles and American bombers. The new missiles tended to have much less destructive capability than either bombers or the Atlas and Titan missiles. Their warheads were about one megaton as compared to perhaps forty megatons carried in a bomber. The missiles had the additional advantage of being both highly accurate and highly controllable in a technical sense, as well as being well protected. This force resulted in the development of a strategy based on confidence that forces could survive the early hours of a nuclear war and could remain under firm control. Technology then made possible what seemed intellectually desirable and what was also to become important for policy reasons.

The general thrust of the Kennedy Administration's military strategy was the development of the doctrines of flexible response and multiple options; that is, the creation of a military force which would remain under tight civilian control at all times and which could be used in a variety of different ways to meet a variety of different threats. Controlled response was simply the part of the flexible-response strategy dealing with nuclear war. An administration which recognized that limited war and guerrilla war could come in a variety of different forms and could require many different kinds of responses also recognized, and wanted to be in a position to deal with, a number of different ways in which general nuclear war might break out. It was important for an administration stressing options and flexible response to be able to say that even strategic forces had been brought under tight control and could be used in different ways according to appropriate policy.

In addition, the Kennedy Administration launched a major attack on European national nuclear forces. It rejected the view of the Eisenhower Administration that the British force made a marginal, but useful, contribution to alliance deterrence. Rather it implied that such forces were wasteful of resources and perhaps dangerous during a crisis. The immediate cause of Mr. McNamara's speech enunciating the controlled-response doctrine was an attempt to justify American opposition to national nuclear forces and to explain them in the context of the need for central control over all nuclear forces before and during a general nuclear war. The doctrine of controlled response provided one motivation for American opposition to national nuclear forces; but, in turn, this opposition provided increased motivation to publicly state a controlled-response doctrine.

These pressures led to the enunciation of a controlled-response strategy by Mr. McNamara at Ann Arbor. While the underlying principles have remained, changes in technology and policy since 1961 have been made. The importance of not attacking Soviet cities is not emphasized as much as the need for the United States to develop a capability of its own to *limit damage* to the United States and to provide *assured destruction* in the Soviet Union in order to deter a nuclear war. Without rejecting the notion that the United States should not hit cities first, recent public statements of the Johnson Administration have stressed the inherent destructiveness and uncontrollability of general nuclear war. Mr. McNamara has also deflated the value of a first strike against Soviet forces in view of the increase in size and protection of the Soviet strategic forces. Rather, the Secretary has asserted the importance of a combination of offensive forces and active and passive defensive forces for the United States, which would provide a capacity to limit damage should war occur. The precise nature of this strategy may vary again as Soviet forces change in size and shape and as innovations in technology occur. But the basic components of controlled response are likely to remain part of the American strategic posture.

COMPONENTS OF
CONTROLLED-RESPONSE STRATEGY

What capability, communication, and action policies are required for the successful implementation of a controlled-response strategy?

The capability required for controlled response, as interpreted by the Johnson Administration, calls for development of well-protected strategic forces capable of surviving not only an enemy first strike but also repeated enemy attacks. Such forces are to be under tight command and control so that they can be used by the top political leadership in a variety of different ways, including the ability to engage in selective attack against a very small number of targets or against a limited class of targets. Such forces must be maintained at a high peak of readiness at all times and able both to move to the highest alert status quickly—and if necessary imperceptively—during a crisis and to hold that status indefinitely.

The size of the force depends upon two objectives: first, a force large enough to enable assured destruction of a significant portion of Soviet industry and population, as a deterrent against Soviet deliberate attack; second, a larger force in order to carry out the damage-limiting role—that is, to reduce insofar as possible whatever damage could be caused to the United States. The size of the force, then, is related to the size of the Soviet strategic force and its vulnerability to an attack.

The necessary size of the strategic offensive forces (SOF) is related to the ability of active defenses, such as fighters, anti-aircraft and anti-missile forces, and passive defenses, such as civil defense, to carry out the same objective of damage limiting. Damage can be limited by destroying enemy strategic forces on the ground; by destroying with air or missile defense, enemy strategic forces before they reach the United States; and finally, by reducing the vulnerability of the American population through the use of fall-out shelters. The construction of such shelters (which was urged by the Administration) would, according to calculations made by the Pentagon in 1964–65, save more lives in the event of a general nuclear war than any other addition to the strategic offensive and defensive forces of the United States. Particularly in a case in which cities were not attacked, the number of lives saved would be very great. The construction of these shelters would limit the number of civilian casualties and would thereby signal American interest in deterrence and in negotiation after a war had begun in order to avoid direct city attacks. Whether ballistic-missile defenses should be procured for damage-limiting purposes has remained a major issue during the 1960's.

An appropriate communication policy for the controlled-response doctrine must alert the Soviet Union to the possibility that the United States will seek to exercise restraint and carry on negotiations after a war begins and also to the fact that the United States has well-protected strategic forces and, consequently, has no need to engage in an inadvertent strike.

American statements have, in fact, asserted that American forces are designed to ride out a Soviet attack; therefore, no American forces would be released for attack on the Soviet Union until a significant number of nuclear weapons had exploded in the United States. In addition, the possibility and desirability of trying to limit a general nuclear war, should one occur, and of terminating the war by negotiations rather than by exhausting the forces on both sides has been emphasized. American statements have continued to focus on the importance of avoiding direct attack on Soviet cities, if the limitation of nuclear war is to have any real meaning.

The actions of the United States have sought to reinforce American statements. The hot-line agreement between the United States and the Soviet Union, in providing for a direct means of communication, both creates the physical possibility of rapid negotiations after the outbreak of nuclear war and perhaps symbolizes the willingness of both sides to engage in such negotiations. The substantial American investment in command and control capabilities also serves to signal an interest in controlled response.

The action policy of the United States in the event of nuclear war will, of course, depend importantly on how the war breaks out. As has been indicated, the Administration prefers not to commit itself to a single action plan prior to the start of a general nuclear war. Nevertheless, the Administration appears to support avoiding initiation of attacks on cities, while at the same time launching—as soon as it is sure that a war has begun—perceptible attacks on all Soviet strategic targets. Presumably the United States would attempt to maintain communication with the Soviet Union and to negotiate an end to the war as soon as possible.

OBJECTIONS TO CONTROLLED RESPONSE

The strategy of controlled response, with its goals of limiting maximum damage in a general nuclear war, while giving first priority to deterring such a war, might seem unobjectionable. In fact, however, the enunciation of the doctrine by Mr. McNamara evoked a storm of criticism in the United States and elsewhere, which has continued. The objections which will be considered here are: the Soviets will not adopt the strategy given their inferiority; the strategy is of no value if both sides have well-protected strategic forces; it is only valuable in a first strike; the strategy increases the danger of an inadvertent nuclear war; and finally, it leads to an accelerated arms race.

Soviet publicists reacted violently to the announcement of the controlled-response doctrine by the United States. They argued that the strategy was an attempt to justify an American first strike; and they implied that the Soviet Union would continue to strike population centers, as well as military targets, in the event of a general nuclear war. Later Soviet statements were more moderate but still rejected the doctrine. It is probably true that as long as the Soviet Union has a much smaller nuclear force than the United States, it will be reluctant to discuss publicly the possibility of eliminating attacks on cities and negotiating an end to a war. Such discussions may appear to reduce the credibility of a Soviet attack and hence make an American attack, at least during crisis, more likely. Nevertheless, even if the Soviets reject the strategy publicly, it is clearly in their interest to seek to limit damage, if war occurs. Such limitation concerns both sides; but it is even more in the interest of the weaker, rather than the stronger, power. Once war begins, the Soviet Union can do much less damage to the United States, even if it attacks American cities, than the United States can do to the Soviet Union, despite the greater concentration of American population. Moreover, the greatest Soviet objective—particularly as long as the Soviet Union is weaker than the United States—is to avoid a general nuclear war.

Another objection to the strategy focuses on striking strategic targets in preference to cities. The objection implies that the strategy does not make sense once both sides have well-protected strategic forces and, even before that, makes sense only in the case of an American first strike. This range of criticisms is aimed particularly at the war-fighting version of the strategy, as stated by Mr. McNamara in June of 1962. However, the objections do not apply to the strategy in general. As the Soviets have hardened and dispersed their strategic force—primarily into submarines—two facts have become clear: first, the United States cannot hope to destroy all, or even most, of the Soviet strategic force in a first strike; secondly, there are some forces which the United States simply cannot or will not attack, because it is too expensive and difficult to do so. For the foreseeable future, though, the Soviets will have a number of strategic targets that can be attacked in an American first, or even second, strike. For example, as long as bombers remain an important part of the Soviet strategic force, it will be possible to attack planes which have not yet taken off, which have returned and are preparing for a second strike, or which are located at refueling bases on their way to the United States. There have been a number of press reports suggesting that at least the first- and second-generation Soviet missiles had a reload capability; that is, the same launcher was equipped to fire a second missile. Obviously these launch sites would remain important strategic targets, even after a Soviet first strike. Finally, defensive targets, such as the radar used with air defense or missile defense, very likely would be struck down in order to maintain the American ability to destroy Soviet cities, should that become necessary.

The critics of the controlled-response doctrine, who have stressed these issues, miss a crucial point: that the alternative to attacking Soviet strategic forces is not to engage in senseless city destruction but rather to withhold the forces and seek to negotiate an end to the nuclear war. In this case, nuclear war is likely to be much slower than has previously been envisioned, and may include very limited strategic strikes and bargaining and communication between the two sides. If a local war is in progress, nuclear war may consist of attacks on other kinds of targets, including tactical military targets, or economic targets, such as oil refineries far from population centers.

Many critics felt that because at least the no-cities version of controlled response seemed to stress the importance of a first strike, such a strategy would increase the danger of an inadvertent general war. This criticism assumed that prior to the adoption of a controlled-response strategy, cities were on the target list and military centers were not. However, it needs to be emphasized that whatever the strategy, both the United States and the Soviet Union would attack, as soon as possible, those strategic forces of their enemy that could be most easily destroyed. Taking cities off the list does not in any way affect the incentive to strike quickly in order to destroy vulnerable strategic targets. Moreover, it is the vulnerability of the strategic forces themselves, and not the attempt to establish control or to avoid cities, that makes an inadvertent strike dangerous. The possibility of first-strike motives influencing decision makers can only be reduced by the development of well-protected strategic forces by one or both sides. To the extent that emphasis on control has contributed to the pressure to develop forces that are well protected and designed to survive a first strike, it serves to reduce the danger of an inadvertent strike.

Finally, it has been argued that a controlled-response strategy will lead to an unaccelerated arms race. However, this criticism confuses an attempt to control general nuclear war, if it occurs, with a commitment to a dominant strategic position for the United States. The United States has in fact recognized for the last several years that if the Soviets did build well-protected strategic forces, the United States could not hope to have the kind of strategic dominance that it had in the 1950's. In fact, the American strategic budget has declined dramatically in the period 1962–65, from approximately fifteen billion dollars a year to six billion dollars a year for strategic offensive forces. This decline and the failure to increase the programmed size of American strategic offensive forces occurred because of the realization that targets for these forces did not exist, despite the adoption of a controlled-response strategy. The offensive arms race will resume if, for technological or political reasons, both sides find it necessary to build active defenses or if some unforeseen technological development occurs. However, it has been demonstrated that a controlled-response doctrine by itself is no bar to a tacit, or even a formal, halt to the strategic arms race.

SELECTED BIBLIOGRAPHY

Brodie, Bernard. *Strategy in the Missile Age.* Princeton, N.J.: Princeton University Press, 1959.

Kahn, Herman. *On Thermonuclear War.* Princeton, N.J.: Princeton University Press, 1960.

_____. *Thinking about the Unthinkable.* New York: Horizon Press, 1962.

Knorr, Klaus, and Thornton Read, eds. *Limited Strategic War.* New York: Frederick A. Praeger, 1962.

Snyder, Glenn H. *Deterrence and Defense.* Princeton, N.J.: Princeton University Press, 1961.

CHAPTER EIGHT

Limited War: The Nature of the Limiting Process

The age of the nuclear missile has been characterized by warfare conducted without the use of modern nuclear
weapons. Local wars—those that do not take place on the homelands of either the United States or the Soviet Union but still
concern the two superpowers—have broken out from time to
time in various parts of the globe. This chapter will examine the
process by which such wars start and by which the superpowers
become involved yet refrain from using their major military capabilities. The following chapters will consider specific policy problems related to the defense of Europe and Asia.

DETERMINANTS OF POLICY

Since the major powers do have much more military force than
they have used in any local war situation, an effort to understand
the limiting process requires an examination of the decision-
making procedures that determine to what extent the major powers
will involve themselves in a local conflict. The determinants of
this policy in terms of objectives, the fear of general war, images
of the role of force, and domestic politics will be examined in turn.

Objectives

The general foreign-policy objectives of the major powers influence the underlying approach of the countries in dealing with attempts by other powers or groups to bring about changes by means of violence. American foreign policy throughout the postwar period has been guided by the objective of "containment." This has meant in practice that the United States would attempt to use a combination of military, political, and economic pressures to prevent the expansion of Communist control, or control by the Soviet Union or Communist China. The United States has also been committed to supporting the United Nations, with its ideal of employing peaceful methods for effecting change. The goal of the non-use of military force has also been espoused directly by the United States. Finally, the United States has supported the objective of bringing about political stability and economic development in the non-Communist areas of the world.

The basic foreign-policy objectives of the Soviet Union and Communist China have been at considerable variance with American objectives, although there has been some change in the Soviet position over the last several years. Nevertheless, the Soviets appear to be interested in expanding the area under Soviet control and under Communist control, except perhaps where that expansion would give an important advantage to the Chinese. Peking remains committed to limiting American influence and military presence—first in Taiwan and then throughout Asia—and thereby expanding Chinese influence in those countries on the periphery. Throughout the world the Chinese have been interested in establishing revolutionary governments.

These broad political objectives, including more recent Soviet interest in international stability and containment of Communist China, have shaped the way in which the major powers have looked upon particular attempts to change international boundaries or domestic political arrangements by the use of force. Nevertheless, partly because they are only using very limited amounts of their military, political, and economic power, none of the superpowers can have any expectation of fulfilling all, or even a substantial part of, their general foreign-policy objectives by conducting a local war. They are thus faced with the problem of relating their specific objectives to their more general and long-range aims.

Because of the relative lack of importance of the actual territories being fought over in limited-war situations, the most important objectives at stake have been the perceived political effects of various possible outcomes. In general, the superpowers have justified their intervention in local conflicts by citing the need to convince other countries that they would be defended if they came under attack. In reacting to the invasion of South Korea in 1950, to the Soviet ultimatums about Berlin in the late 1950's and early 1960's, to the Cuban missile crisis, and to the Vietcong threat in South Vietnam, the United States has been motivated—at least in part—by the belief that it could further deter Soviet or Chinese military moves only by intervening and thus establishing the credibility of its guarantee to other countries.

In many situations the United States has been more concerned with the lessons which its allies and other countries would draw from its actions than what was communicated to enemies. For example, American actions in Korea were carried out with an eye towards the reaction of Japan and America's NATO allies, if Korea had been allowed to fall. Similarly, the defense of Vietnam has been justified on grounds that the Thais and others would accommodate China unless the United States showed in South Vietnam that it was prepared to defend them. This justification is sometimes discussed in terms of the "falling-dominos" theory, which is based on the premise that if one country falls, all of the other countries—at least in the area—would also fall to Communist control. Viewed mechanically and literally, the falling-dominos image is obviously wrong; but the fact that it would be harder for the United States to convince other allies of its commitment to defend them, if the United States permitted one country to be taken by military violence, seems clear. In any case, the calculation of political effects, in providing motivation for attempting to win a local war or at least for preventing the successful use of violence, has proved to be an important influence on American policy makers.

Other pressures have worked in the opposite direction. At least until 1965 the United States appeared to give the highest priority to the buildup of American and Allied forces on the ground in

Central Europe. It sought to use crises such as the Korean War to stimulate an increase in European defense efforts and was willing for this reason, and also because it feared that Korea might be a feint before Soviet attack in Europe, to increase substantially American strength in Europe while the Korean War was still going on. While all of America's allies are prepared to defend the principle that the United States should use force to prevent Communist take-overs, there has been much disagreement over specific use of American military power. The unhappiness with American policy in such areas as the Taiwan Strait—over the defense of the islands of Quemoy and Matsu—has generated pressures to reduce the American military involvement in these areas, perhaps even at the expense of a less successful defense of the area under attack.

The objectives of the Soviet Union and Communist China have been to create political effects which are the reverse of those sought by the United States. Thus, the two Communist powers are interested in demonstrating a general American weakness and lack of will or—in the words of the Chinese—that the United States is a "paper tiger," which must be tactically respected, although strategically despised. Both the Soviets and the Chinese have also tried to demonstrate the power and capability of their countries; in particular, Peking has been committed to demonstrating the efficacy of supporting what it would call wars of national liberation.

The relationships between the political effects sought in fighting a locally limited war, the territorial objectives pursued, and the war-termination conditions which are acceptable, have always been extremely difficult to calculate. As a result, there have been fluctuations and uncertainty in the war-termination conditions set by the superpowers. In the Korean War, for example, American objectives fluctuated all the way from defending South Korea to capturing all of Korea, while the Soviets and Chinese were at one time seeking to capture all of Korea, at another, simply defending part of North Korea. Since a superpower tries to gauge, to some extent, contradictory reactions of various governments and peoples, there is no easy way of establishing the precise relation between one set of conditions terminating local war and another, and the political effects sought. Nevertheless, this attempt is made and determines the willingness of the superpowers to invest greater material effort to win a local war or leads them to seek an early termination of the conflict.

The Fear of General War

There is a widespread belief, which has apparently been shared by leaders in the Soviet Union, the United States, and—despite their statements to the contrary—Communist China, that the possibility of a general nuclear war increases during a local war. This fear—referred to in the West as the danger of "escalation" and by the Soviet Union as the danger of "a single spark" leading to a general nuclear war—has had a major impact on the decisions of the superpowers in relation to local wars and crises.

In examining the question of how a general nuclear war might arise from a local war, we must return to the two kinds of "escalation" (discussed in Chapter Two): expansion and explosion. In the process of expansion, local war—and this might especially apply to a local war in Europe—might increase gradually in size until, almost imperceptively, it would become a general nuclear war involving attacks on the homelands of the Soviet Union and the United States. Alternatively, a local war, even a very low-level military clash, could suddenly explode into general nuclear war either because of fears of an inadvertent strike on both sides or because one side or the other had deliberately decided to unleash nuclear war as a result of setbacks on the local battlefield.

The desire of the superpowers to avoid general nuclear war has been a major influence on the foreign policy of the United States, the Soviet Union, and Communist China, throughout the entire postwar period. Probably, leaders of these countries have had no clear image of how a general nuclear war might arise out of a local war, but they have recognized that the growing tension and increased use of military force could somehow get out of hand and lead to a nuclear conflict which nobody wanted. They have realized that when decisions have to be made more quickly, when troops have to be authorized to make some decisions locally, and when tensions and political conflicts heighten, events may no longer be under the complete control of political leaders and may generate pressures leading to a nuclear war.

It is impossible to specify, either in general or for any historical event, how close the world actually has been to nuclear war or even just what it means to say that the world has moved closer to a nuclear war. Nevertheless, it appears that political leaders, because of the destructive nature of nuclear war, have tended to overestimate the probability that nuclear war would develop from any particular local crisis and, for that reason, have been less willing to commit military forces than they might otherwise be.

China, the United States, and the Soviet Union have all sought to manipulate the fear of general nuclear war in order to get advantages in a local conflict. However, with the exception of the Cuban missile crisis, there has been little explicit effort to exploit the particular nature of the strategic balance.

Images of the Role of Force

The way a country and its leaders look at international politics and their notions of what is proper and improper behavior have an important impact on what policies they pursue and what actions they seek to prevent. In particular, images of the role that force can—and should—play in international politics influences the behavior of the United States, the Soviet Union, and Communist China.

The United States is committed to the principle that force should not be used to settle political issues. Moreover, the United States believes that it has an obligation to prevent the use of force, particularly in changing international boundaries or the government of a country by outside military pressure. Virtually all American leaders—and certainly all who have been leaders since the Second World War—reject the notion that force should be used offensively by the United States to seek to change boundaries or alter control of governments. Although this principle has been violated on several occasions, there is a belief that only as much force as is necessary should be used to resist opposing forces. As President Johnson put it, the response should be measured, related to the provocation, and as limited as possible— at least partly because of the humanitarian desire to avoid destruction.

There have been other ideas about the role of force that have been widely held among dissenting American elites. Perhaps the most important of these is the belief that a clear moral and legal issue is needed to justify the use of violence. This range of concerns has influenced those who have criticized American involvement in Vietnam on the grounds that its legal and moral justifications are shaky and that the desire to prevent a Communist takeover in South Vietnam is simply not enough to overcome the restrictions which should be put on the American use of military force. At the other end are those that argue that the United States should only intervene if it is committed to "victory"—and at least in the early postwar period that meant victory over its major opponent. Thus, many objected to American conduct in the Korean War because the United States was committed to a "no-win" policy.

The Soviet Union and Communist China, on the other hand, have looked upon force as a legitimate instrument of policy to be used interchangeably with other means in order to expand the area under Communist control. Furthermore, a perceived belief in the importance of probing the enemy and testing his willingness to resist the use of force and in seeking to use as much force as can be successfully applied has evolved. Finally, the leaders of both countries have stressed the importance of political control over the use of military force.

Domestic Policies

There is a popular belief in the United States that politics should stop at the border: that there should not be domestic political conflict over foreign-policy issues. Equally popular is the notion that in Communist societies foreign policy can be carried out without reference to domestic political considerations. In fact, however, domestic political considerations have played, and are likely to continue to play, a major role in determining policy on limited-war questions in the Soviet Union, Communist China, and the United States. While general war or even a very large-scale conventional war could lead to the suspension of domestic political conflict, evidence from the Korean War and the war in Vietnam makes it clear that the conduct of a limited war would become an important domestic political issue and would be influenced by domestic political considerations. This is true, if for no other reason than that local wars require the use of scarce resources—resources that might otherwise be allocated for internal development or for other foreign-policy activities. Therefore, the conduct of a war must be intimately related to general conflicts within the society about the correct and desirable allocation of resources. Certainly American policy in Vietnam—in particular the widespread effort since 1965 to demonstrate that the United States wishes to negotiate—is influenced by domestic criticism of the policy and by the desire of the President to assuage his domestic opponents. President Johnson's interest in promoting a Great Society influences his actions as did Truman's interest in the New Deal. Similarly in the Soviet Union, and perhaps to a lesser extent in Communist China, the proper role of the country in various local conflicts has been tied up with problems of succession and also problems of policy.

THE LIMITING PROCESS

We have examined the objectives that determine both whether or not a superpower will enter into a local war and, if it does enter into war, the extent of its involvement. We turn now to an analysis of the *limiting process*: the process by which local wars begin to settle on certain limits and are brought to an end.

If a nuclear war begins, it will be because of the deliberate decision by one of a very few number of decision centers to use the weapons or at least to release them to troop commanders who can then make the decision to use them. Thus, deterrence of a general nuclear war can focus on decision makers in Washington and Moscow. However, a local war can break out from a number of different causes; it can result from the decisions of a large number of different decision centers. Some of the local wars in the postwar period have erupted because of the deliberate decision by a Communist state to try to bring about change through the use of force. Korea, for example, resulted from a deliberate North Korean and Soviet decision. Or decisions made by groups in the local area—local Communist parties or local non-Communist groups or countries—may initiate local war. Finally, the United States might decide to begin a local war.

A local war is by definition limited. The limits that have been observed, and may be carried out in future local wars, can be considered in terms of geography, targets, weapons, and the degree of participation of various states.

The geographic area in which local wars have been fought in the postwar period has been rather small; for example, the Korean War was limited to the Korean Peninsula, the Cuban missile crisis to Cuba and the water surrounding it, the war in Vietnam to North and South Vietnam and the surrounding waters.

Even within the area of combat both countries have observed limitations on targets attacked, particularly by airpower. The United States observed a whole series of different limitations during the Korean War. In the initial stages it attacked only military targets in North Korea; later it extended the area under attack to industrial targets, but not those close to the Soviet and Chinese borders. Then restrictions on attacks close to the Chinese border were removed. The Chinese, on the other hand, engaged in no bombing at all in South Korea except for some minor heckling raids. In Vietnam, again, the United States observed a varying series of limitations on the targets which it would attack in North and South Vietnam.

Not using nuclear weapons has been perhaps the most significant limitation which has been adhered to by the superpowers. The reasons for this restraint on the part of the United States and the Soviet Union have varied over time. One reason has been the belief that the use of any nuclear weapons in a local conflict would make general nuclear war more likely. A second belief holds that the use of these weapons would be extremely unpopular in other countries of the world. At the time of the Korean War, the United States had a relatively small supply of nuclear weapons and was inhibited by the desire not to use up forces that were seen as the major deterrent to possible Soviet moves elsewhere in the world, particularly in Europe. There was also little understanding of the actual uses to which nuclear weapons could be put in tactical situations. Neither the United States nor the Soviet Union now have any real shortage of nuclear capability, and both have developed much more sophisticated nuclear weapons of various sizes and weapons effects. Nevertheless, the political costs of using nuclear weapons seem even greater, as does the danger that the use of nuclear weapons will make general war more likely.

Other limitations on weapons have been observed by various countries in particular limited wars. No countries have, for example, used biological or chemical weapons; and the Chinese Communists and the Russians have refrained from introducing various kinds of weaponry, including submarines and bombers, into a number of limited-war situations.

The degree of participation of the superpowers in any local-war situation can vary all the way from virtual indifference or failure to take sides, as the Soviets did during the Indo-Pakistani clash in 1965, to direct involvement of combat troops, for example, on the part of the United States in Korea and later in Vietnam. The points in between can range from active diplomatic aid, through the sending of military supplies and technicians, through the use of volunteers or advisers in a more active combat role.

Thus far in our discussion of the limiting process and local war, we have considered the pressures on decision makers to become involved in local conflicts but also to limit their commitment. We have also examined the kinds of limitations which might be, and have been, observed in local-war situations. It remains to be asked: Are there any general statements which can be made about why limited wars take the course they actually do, why certain limits are observed and not others, and why war terminates in the way that it does?

Some generalizations can be made, but perhaps the most important one is: The specifics of any limited-war situation will determine that encounter. The explanation for any limited war is to be seen much less as a consequence of some general propositions about limiting war in the Nuclear Age and much more as a result of the specific international and local political factors.

Limits are carried out, not because of any agreement, whether tacit or formal, between the countries concerned, but because of decisions made within various countries. Therefore, it has been emphasized that to understand limited war we need to look not only at the interaction between states but also at the internal decision-making processes.

Events since 1949 have demonstrated repeatedly what many analysts continued to doubt into the 1950's; namely, that limited wars were possible: that superpowers, whether democracies or dictatorships, could be involved in military conflicts with significant numbers of casualties and still refrain from attacking the homeland of the opposing superpower. Limiting their involvement has also included stopping somewhere short of the use of their major weapons systems and stopping in a way which does not force their opponent to use all of its military power.

The limits that have been observed result, as has been stressed, from domestic decision-making processes; these limits can be catalogued from an international perspective. It is clear that some of the limits are symmetrical; that is, both sides refrain from doing the same things. Some may even result from conscious bargaining and interaction. However, many others are not symmetrical—one side refrains from doing something which the other side is doing —and many are not based on any conscious bargaining process or recognition of likely reactions. Many limits are actually based on misunderstandings, misconceptions, or at least different perceptions of what is taking place. Others may be based on negotiating and bargaining with allies or with other countries rather than with the enemy.

The initiation of a local conflict is frequently not deliberate; certainly fighting is not always started because of a deliberate decision by one of the superpowers. A local conflict may also be terminated for reasons unrelated to the interest of the superpowers and frequently for reasons unrelated to the local battlefield outcome.

Finally, it should be noted that it is very difficult to judge who won a local war. If both sides are fighting mainly because of the political effects of winning or losing, the relevant questions become: What are the political effects in specific situations, and how might they be changed by additional efforts on the battlefield? The answers to these questions plague historians and political analysts as much as they do policy makers at the time. What, for example, would have been the consequences of permitting North Korea to overrun South Korea or, on the other hand, the consequences of carrying the war to China and capturing all of North Korea? What actually would be the consequences of permitting Quemoy or even Berlin to be taken over by the Communists? What gains did the United States make from the successful defense of Quemoy in 1958? These are difficult questions to answer, even in retrospect, and were much more difficult to deal with at the time. Because of these uncertainties, because there are no clear answers, the decisions taken by various countries will be affected by a whole range of different factors—some directly relevant to the situation, some not. A general understanding of the limiting process can be useful in considering particular situations and in determining policy for the direct defense of local areas, but it is only a very small part of what we need to know.

SELECTED BIBLIOGRAPHY

Halperin, Morton H. *Limited War in the Nuclear Age.* New York: John Wiley & Sons, 1963.

Kissinger, Henry A. *Nuclear Weapons and Foreign Policy.* New York: Harper, 1957.

Osgood, Robert E. *Limited War: The Challenge to American Strategy.* Chicago: University of Chicago Press, 1957.

CHAPTER NINE

Deterrence and
Defense in Europe

The NATO alliance was formed in 1949 because of the belief that the Soviet Union might attempt a military move in Central Europe within the next few years. There had been a widespread fear that such an attack would occur during the time of the Berlin blockade in 1948; and fears were expressed again following the outbreak of the Korean War in June, 1950. During the early years, all the members of the Alliance shared the views that war was extremely likely, that it could be deterred only by a substantial buildup of alliance forces, and that one had to be ready to fight. During the course of the 1950's the belief in the imminence of war in Europe declined slowly but steadily, so that by the end of the decade it was thought that war in Europe was extremely unlikely. Many attributed this change to the military strength of NATO; therefore, it was thought necessary to maintain this force and to develop a strategy consistent with the belief that war in Europe was improbable but that the residual possibility of war did exist.

At the same time, increased attention was given to the problems of political relations within the Alliance. This chapter will examine the problem of deterring, or defending against, a Soviet military attack; the following chapter will deal with political arrangements for the control of nuclear weapons.

THE SOVIET MILITARY THREAT

Though all forms of military action in the NATO area are believed to be unlikely, it is recognized that history consists of the occurrence of the unlikely and, in many cases, the occurrence of unforeseen events; therefore, the forces of the NATO alliance must plan for possible contingencies. This planning begins with an attempt to assess the range of possible Soviet military threats. The most serious, if also perhaps the most improbable, Soviet threat would be the initiation of large-scale ground war on the central front. An all-out attack on the central front, a Soviet attempt to reach the channel as quickly as possible—this was the image of warfare that guided the formation of NATO but that, over time, seems more and more unreal. Short of an all-out attack, the Soviets might use their forces for a probe—an attempt to discover whether NATO would be willing to react militarily—perhaps by seizing a piece of territory. Such a probe could conceivably occur on the central front, most probably in Berlin but possibly in other cities such as Hamburg; on the northern front on the northern cap of Norway; or on the southern front in the area of Greece and Turkey.

Moving down the scale of violence from the overt use of military force, the Soviets have employed their military capability for political purposes. They have engaged in some limited forms of nuclear blackmail; for example, threatening to destroy any air base from which an American U-2 plane took off. They might engage in more drastic acts of nuclear blackmail, such as ordering a country to withdraw from the NATO alliance or to suffer the consequence—a nuclear attack. Short of this blackmail, the Soviets have used the presence of their large military forces in Central Europe as a form of military pressure which has affected the political discussions about the future of Central Europe. Finally, the Soviets have employed their military force on their own side of the Iron Curtain: their large-scale effort occurred in 1956, when Soviet troops squelched the Hungarian Revolution. There appears to be a tacit understanding, confirmed in 1956, that NATO would not interfere in cases of military action in Eastern Europe.

The Soviet Union has restricted itself to lower-level military actions; it will probably continue to do so. However, more severe actions, if carried out, would result in very great cost to the

West. Thus the NATO alliance has to decide what threats it wants to be able to deal with and how it will deal with them.

Must we prepare for events perceived to be extremely unlikely? Some Europeans and Americans, viewing any military action in Central Europe as improbable, conclude that only very small military forces are needed in Europe; others, however, would argue that a limited probe, such as an attempt to seize Hamburg, is even more unlikely and less worth preparing for. There is also the question of how far NATO interests extend. Do they extend, for example, to Yugoslavia or to the countries of Eastern Europe? As various countries in Eastern Europe move more and more out of direct Soviet control, an issue which appeared to be settled in 1956 may arise again: Should NATO have the capability to prevent the Soviet use of military force beyond Soviet borders?

What threats are to be met is related to the appropriate strategies for dealing with these threats: what is perceived as likely to occur and the cost involved in preparing for these contingencies. We turn then to an examination of alternative NATO strategies.

ALTERNATIVE NATO STRATEGIES

This section considers in some detail each of several strategies that have been proposed for the defense of the NATO area. These include massive retaliation, the instant use of tactical nuclear weapons, the pause, and conventional defense. These strategies have generally been considered in terms of their effect in deterring an attack on the central front. However, our assumption is that it is necessary to consider these alternatives, not only in relation to deterrence, but also in case deterrence fails and the use of military force is needed. The economic and domestic political costs of various strategies for different countries must also be weighed. Each strategy will be discussed in turn, both in terms of capability, communication, and action policies and its value in dealing with Soviet threats in Europe.

Massive Retaliation

The strategy of massive retaliation is based on the threat of instant and massive use of strategic nuclear power by the West, particularly that of the United States against the Soviet Union in the event of Soviet aggression in Europe. This strategy, which was the basis of NATO planning—at least until 1954 when the emphasis was put on tactical nuclear weapons—requires no ground forces. Since the strategic nuclear power is to be used immediately against the Soviet Union, there appears to be no need for forces that would directly defend against the Soviet attack. Nevertheless, it has always been argued that a number of ground troops is needed. In the earliest postwar years there was some doubt as to whether the nuclear power of the Alliance was sufficient to quell a Soviet attack. It was believed that even after all American weapons—what by current standards was a limited stock—had been used, the Soviet Army might continue to advance. Even after this no longer seemed possible, because of the very large strategic stockpile belonging to the United States, some ground troops were thought necessary to establish the fact that aggression had taken place. Terms such as "plate-glass window" and "trip-wire" were used to express the notion that troops on the ground, including American troops, would serve the function of signaling that aggression had, in fact, taken place. The enemy would be forced to destroy these troops, thus "breaking the glass" or "tripping the wire" and bringing into play the American strategic force. Finally, and perhaps most important, the presence of American ground troops in Europe has been seen as necessary to affirm the political guarantee of the United States. The American military divisions in Europe are a way of providing a hostage force to demonstrate the American commitment to Europe and to make more credible the use of nuclear weapons by the United States in the defense of Europe. Consequently, if the United States were to station large numbers of troops on the central front, it was believed necessary to have a corresponding number of European ground troops, even if the purpose of the American troops was largely to symbolize the American commitment.

The threat of the use of massive strategic nuclear weapons seems to have in fact been sufficient, if not necessary, to deter a full-scale Soviet attack on the central front. The Soviets may never have planned such an attack; but, assuming that they had at least contemplated such action, the possibility that it would lead to a general nuclear war was probably sufficient in the past and will remain sufficient in the future to deter the attack. However, the threat of massive retaliation has proved unsuccessful and unsatisfactory in dealing with lesser threats, including the various Soviet moves against Berlin.

Clearly, the strategy of massive retaliation would be unsatisfactory if deterrence failed. If war did break out in Europe—either because of a deliberate Soviet decision on the assumption that American military power would not be used or if a large-scale war were to grow out of, for example, an uprising in Eastern Germany—massive retaliation would not be the desired strategy to use. Once war began, some alternative options before resorting to the strategic nuclear power of the Alliance would be needed. There are few, if any, commentators or officials who consider massive retaliation an acceptable action policy and only a small number who consider it even a satisfactory communication policy. Thus, there has been a search for alternatives that would provide for ground forces in Europe for dealing with at least the initial stages of a Soviet attack.

Tactical Nuclear Weapons

In the mid-1950's the United States began to develop an arsenal of sophisticated and varied tactical nuclear weapons. At the same time it had become evident that the countries of the NATO alliance were not going to raise enough ground forces to deal directly with a Soviet threat. Thus, as the fear that nuclear weapons alone would not be sufficient to deter the Soviet Union gave way to the belief that relying only on strategic nuclear weapons was not the most advisable plan, tactical nuclear weapons became the only solution. This strategy, which was adopted formally by the NATO Council in 1957, called for ground forces of significant size, perhaps thirty divisions on the central front, equipped with tactical nuclear weapons. Planning was based on the assumption that the use of these weapons would be authorized immediately if an attack occurred; thus, planning was only for tactical or strategic nuclear war. This is the strategy that continues to be favored by most NATO military planners and by several European governments, particularly the Federal Republic of Germany.

This strategy assumes that any action on the central front would be a major military move deliberately taken by the Soviet Union and hence an action significant enough to justify the introduction of nuclear weapons by the West. It assumes also that it is clearly to the advantage of the West to use tactical nuclear weapons in the event of local ground warfare. This is a question which has been debated widely with inconclusive results, but there is a growing consensus on the proposition that the use of tactical nuclear weapons is not necessarily an advantage to the West nor does it reduce the manpower needed to deal with a given enemy force. Some analysts, however, would argue that the use of nuclear weapons is an advantage to the West: that the West has and will continue to have a substantial lead in the development of tactical nuclear weapons and hence can fight more effectively with these weapons. Those who advocate a tactical nuclear defense of Europe tend to share some of these views about the advantage of using nuclear weapons and take one of two attitudes towards a conventional defense. They either argue that it is impossible, given the very large Soviet conventional forces, or they argue that an emphasis on conventional forces is undesirable, since it reduces the credibility of the deterrent value of nuclear weapons and hence makes war more likely. In order to come to grips with the question of the value of the use of tactical nuclear weapons, it is necessary to examine several views of what a tactical nuclear war might be like. We will examine four images of tactical nuclear war in Europe; with each image the use of these weapons increases.

The first image is the use of tactical nuclear weapons essentially in a warning, or so-called "shot-across-the-bow," role. It assumes that any use of nuclear weapons would lead very quickly to large-scale nuclear war or to peace. Therefore, the very small-scale use of these weapons, carrying the threat of explosion into general nuclear war, would lead both sides to agree quickly to halt military operations. The advocates of this strategy believe that in the event of an outbreak of military operations, NATO should order the firing of a single nuclear weapon or successive ones to demonstrate its resolve, seriousness, and willingness to risk general nuclear war. Some advocates of this strategy would argue that this single shot should be directed at a tactical military target in the area of operations. Others contend that it should be directed at an industrial or economic target, either in Eastern Europe or perhaps in the Soviet Union. The success of this strategy depends on

two assumptions, both of which appear to be doubtful. The first
is that the resolve of the NATO alliance will be stronger than
that of the Soviet Union. It is difficult to believe, however, that
once an action is taken which increases the risk of nuclear war,
the bargaining position of the NATO alliance will cause the
Soviet Union to be more willing to negotiate on reasonable terms
than it was before the nuclear weapon was used. The strategy
assumes also that the negotiations, regardless of the resolve of the
two parties, could settle on something other than the existing
status quo on the battlefield and specifically that it could settle on
a return to the *status quo ante*. However, in a situation in which
the pressure to negotiate stems from the belief that general nuclear war is about to break out, it appears extremely doubtful that
one can negotiate a return to the *status quo ante*. In fact, the use
of nuclear weapons to demonstrate resolve may most likely lead
to a breakup of the NATO alliance and a willingness on the part
of some countries to settle on terms that seem disastrous to others.

A second image of tactical nuclear war assumes that the use of
nuclear weapons would be confined to very low-yield, sub-kiloton
weapons and to the immediate battlefield area. In such a case,
civilian casualties could be held at relatively low levels, not significantly higher then those of a conventional war. However, the
effect on the battlefield is largely uncertain. The use of such weapons, for example, may make offensive breakthroughs much easier.
In general, in a conventional war it is believed that one must have
a superiority of approximately three to one in a particular area in
order to make a major advance on the ground. The use of tactical
nuclear weapons could substitute for conventional firepower and
make breakthroughs possible with much smaller ratios of offensive to defensive forces. The use of such weapons could also lead
to a total collapse of the armies in the field, resulting in a freezing of the status quo, at the time at which tactical nuclear weapons are used. If both sides fear the introduction of tactical nuclear weapons, strong urges to launch an inadvertent strike are
likely to develop both locally and throughout the theater, or area
of battle, since the first use of these weapons could succeed in
destroying large numbers of troops and equipment which are
not protected against the possibility of a nuclear attack. Forces
ready for nuclear attack would have to be more effectively pro-

tected. This instability not only increases the probability that tactical nuclear weapons might be introduced but also forces troops fighting conventionally to consider at least the need to fight in a way that assumes that tactical nuclear weapons may be used at any time.

A tactical nuclear war being fought with low-yield weapons confined to the battlefield would be extremely unstable. Pressures to expand the war by using larger weapons from beyond the battlefield and attacking logistics lines leading into the battlefield are likely to be very great and, if yielded to, can result in enemy attacks on these weapons systems—on the airbases and missile sites from which weapons are being launched into battle. These actions could very quickly result in the theater use of nuclear weapons discussed below.

Those who believe that a tactical nuclear war might be confined to very small weapons and that such a war is in any case worth preparing for are still faced with the problem of what kinds of nuclear weapons would be most effective in a narrow, tactical, military sense for such an encounter and which weapons would be most effective in preventing the expansion of the tactical nuclear war. A number of studies have been conducted attempting to answer these questions, but the essential uncertainties about tactical nuclear war and the reaction of military forces to this type of war have made it impossible to develop any consensus on these questions.

Tactical nuclear war may involve the use of much larger nuclear weapons, including weapons in the megaton weight range, over the whole theater of military operations. Nuclear weapons may initially be introduced on this scale or after the battlefield use of nuclear weapons described above. Such a use would mean very large civilian casualties, virtually equaling the complete destruction and devastation of Europe. The use of nuclear weapons on this sort of scale is proposed mainly as a deterrent and not as an action policy for the NATO alliance.

In the final image of tactical nuclear war the assumption is made that any war in Europe would lead automatically to worldwide nuclear war in which theater operations—even theater operations in Europe—would not be critical and in which the focus of action would be the strategic interchange between the United States and the Soviet Union.

The Pause

During the late 1950's a number of NATO strategists, including the Supreme Allied Commander in Europe, General Lawrence Norstad, began to be uneasy about strategies that called for the early introduction of tactical nuclear weapons. These strategists feared, on the one hand, that the authorization to use nuclear weapons would not come quickly enough to permit the implementation of the strategy and, on the other, that the use of tactical nuclear weapons would not necessarily be to the advantage of the West. Because of the necessary delay in getting the political authority to use nuclear weapons, it was argued that a pause would inevitably take place: that there would be a period of time during which the West would try to hold the Soviet advance with conventional weapons before nuclear weapons would be used. The question was raised: If some delay were inevitable, should this delay be lengthened so that it would exceed the time necessary to get authority to use nuclear weapons and would be measured in hours or even days during which an end to the fighting could be negotiated? This policy, which appears to be the current NATO action policy, is not the policy for which capabilities are designed nor which NATO attempts to communicate to the enemy.

The strategy assumes that war breaks out either through accident or inadvertence or because of Soviet miscalculation of NATO intentions. Implicit in this strategy, then, is the belief that if the use of nuclear weapons can be delayed for several days, the use will no longer be necessary. However, even in these cases the pause strategy raises a number of questions. Negotiations during a pause, like those following a shot-across-the-bow use of tactical nuclear weapons, are likely to lead at best to a freezing of the status quo at the current battle lines. In both cases the Soviets will be in a strong position, knowing that the West will be faced at the end of the period with the choice of defeat or a large-scale use of tactical nuclear weapons. The pause has a built-in deadline: after the period the NATO alliance must use nuclear weapons, which it has demonstrated a reluctance to use, or face the collapse of its conventional troops. In this situation, negotiations may well lead to a breakup of the alliance over peace terms or over the proper way to use nuclear weapons, resulting in increased Soviet strength.

The decision to introduce nuclear weapons after a pause assumes that, in general, introduction of these weapons would help the West, in which case it is not clear why they have not been used from the outset, at least as soon as permission could be obtained. In any case, there is great uncertainty and great danger of explosion into general nuclear war. The use of battlefield weapons after Soviet advances during the period of a pause is most likely to freeze Soviet gains. Finally, the theater use of nuclear weapons can be most profitable before the Soviets bring up reinforcements; that is, the use of these weapons in an interdictory role to cut off Soviet supplies of troops and ammunition appears to be most effective. Once substantial numbers of Soviet reinforcements have been brought up, it is not certain that even the use of excessive numbers of nuclear weapons would be of value to the West.

Conventional Defense

Dissatisfactions with strategies that rely on the use of tactical nuclear weapons have led to a growing interest, at least in the United States, in strategies which depend to some extent on the use of conventional weapons. Proponents of conventional defense stress two different kinds of strategy: conventional options for at least some contingencies and a complete conventional defense against even an all-out Soviet conventional attack. For both of these kinds of strategy, forces equipped and trained to fight without resorting to nuclear weapons are needed. The advocates of conventional defense want the Soviet Union to believe that this force might be used conventionally, and they state the importance of actually having plans to fight conventionally under a wide range of circumstances. This strategy not only stresses the limitations of the use of tactical nuclear weapons but also maintains that minor Soviet probes or Western offensive actions are the most likely contingencies to be faced in Europe and that the Soviet Union might not introduce nuclear weapons in these cases.

Those who call for conventional options for only certain contingencies hold that the limited option is sufficient to deal with the most likely threats, including limited probes on the Soviet side of the Iron Curtain or inadvertent outbreaks of action. This position recommends the development of a highly mobile force of perhaps four or five divisions that could be rapidly employed on either the northern or the southern flank, as well as on the central front.

Advocates of an all-out conventional defense of Europe argue that a conventional defense is feasible. They point out that Soviet strength has been overestimated, that in fact NATO has more men under arms in Europe than does the Soviet Union and its Warsaw Pact allies, and that with only a marginal increase in effort it would be possible to have a force capable of dealing with any Soviet threat. There would be a need to provide modern conventional equipment for these forces, to relocate the forces, to improve their logistics, and to spend money preparing for a major conventional war rather than, as NATO has in the past, for a major theater nuclear war. In this case, expenditures for air defense and for the protection of military equipment would be with an eye towards a large conventional war rather than a nuclear war. An increase in the number of divisions and a reserve capability commensurate with that of the Soviet Union would also be important.

This approach accepts that an all-out Soviet attack is unlikely, but it points out that the consequences of such an attack are deleterious enough to make the relatively modest investment necessary for dealing with this contingency appear desirable, particularly in light of the unattractiveness of a nuclear defense. Advocates of this view point out that NATO is unlikely to employ any mobile force which it creates unless it is confident that it can hold onto the central front without introducing nuclear weapons. This kind of capability, it is argued, would have important political effects in Central Europe and would make possible a more active political posture aimed at both increasing the freedom of maneuver of East European countries and giving the West a better bargaining position in Berlin.

Those recommending either a conventional option or a total conventional capability dispute the argument that the stress on conventional forces would decrease deterrence; rather, they hold that the probability of using nuclear weapons would remain sufficiently high so that deterrence would not decline appreciably, if at all, for this reason. In addition, the existence of a conventional capability would make intervention by the West more credible and hence might actually increase deterrence.

EVALUATING ALTERNATIVES

During its existence, the NATO alliance has adopted several of the alternative strategies discussed above. Its current policy appears to be some combination of a pause and the development of a conventional option for limited contingencies. In attempting to evaluate these alternatives, the United States must consider its estimate of what the Soviet Union will do as well as how much it is willing to pay in economic and social terms for increased security and higher insurance against unlikely events. Of importance also is the question of whether the NATO alliance should be in a position to react to events on the other side of the Iron Curtain. There is no obvious "technical" answer to what is the best strategy for deterring and defending against Soviet aggression in Europe. The strategy that does emerge from NATO discussions will be as much affected by problems within the Alliance (discussed in the next chapter) as it will be by analysis of the Soviet threat. As belief in the Soviet threat continues to decline, the military forces will appear to play a greater role in intra-alliance issues rather than vis-à-vis the enemy.

SELECTED BIBLIOGRAPHY

Heilbrun, Otto. *Conventional Warfare in the Nuclear Age.* New York: Frederick A. Praeger, 1965.

Richardson, James L. *Germany and the Atlantic Alliance.* Cambridge, Mass.: Harvard University Press, 1966.

Stanley, Timothy W. *NATO in Transition.* New York: Frederick A. Praeger, 1965.

CHAPTER TEN

NATO Nuclear Relations

With the exception of problems raised by Soviet threats to Berlin, which by and large have been handled outside of formal NATO channels, the attention of the United States and its European allies has been focused recently on the complexities of political relationships within the Alliance. The problem has been keeping the Alliance together in order to promote its primary objective of deterring Soviet aggression and at the same time to further "positive" objectives in the economic, social, and political fields. The major conflicts in Europe have been over French proposals to end military integration, arms control, German reunification, and the control over the Alliance's nuclear weapons.

This chapter will deal specifically with the conflict over control of the Alliance's nuclear weapons. A number of different proposals have been offered from time to time by governments and by private analysts to solve the problems created by differences over the control of nuclear weapons within the NATO alliance. The most well-publicized of these proposals was the plan for a multilateral force (MLF) espoused by the United States with varying degrees of enthusiasm from 1960 to 1965. The plan, as originally put forward in the closing days of the Eisenhower Administration, called for the creation of a fleet of Polaris submarines carrying nuclear missiles that would be jointly financed and jointly controlled by all the members of the NATO alliance that desired to participate. The force would be under the control of an MLF control board on which the United States would have a veto. It was assumed also that some combination of European nations would have a veto on the firing of the force.

In its opening days the Kennedy Administration tended to downgrade proposals for nuclear-sharing arrangements, emphasizing instead that first priority should be given to an increase in NATO conventional forces. However, after the signing of the Nassau Agreement between President Kennedy and Prime Minister Harold Macmillan of Great Britain in 1962, the American government began to press for a multilateral force. The proposal for the MLF had by then undergone a change; the United States was now suggesting that the force consist of twenty-five surface ships each equipped with eight Polaris-type missiles. These ships were still to be jointly manufactured, owned, and controlled; however, the control procedures were left open except for the fact that there would be an American veto.

Following its election to office in 1965, the new British Labour Government under Harold Wilson proposed an allied nuclear force (ANF) that combined some of the elements of the MLF with other proposals for placing existing national nuclear forces under the control of NATO. Under the ANF proposal the British V bombers and perhaps the future British Polaris submarines would be turned over to the ANF and would count as the British contribution to the force. Part of the American strategic force would also be included in the ANF. In addition, a new force, considerably smaller than the twenty-five surface ships proposed for the MLF, might be created. This new force would be financed by West Germany and other non-nuclear powers in the ANF arrangement. All the forces would be owned by the ANF countries as a group and could not be used for national purposes.

Soon after the British proposal was made, the United States began to move away from active support for any kind of nuclear-sharing arrangement in Europe and stated, as it had in the early sixties, that it was interested in such a force only if the Europeans demanded it and were able to come up with a joint position.

It now seems clear that if any allied nuclear force is created, it will be very different from either the MLF or ANF and perhaps will involve shared ownership of American-built missiles. However, a *hardware solution*—as such proposals are now termed—is still being considered. Whatever kind of solution is proposed, the NATO alliance—still remains the same. An analysis of the advantages and disadvantages of the MLF and ANF should serve as a useful way of discussing this problem.

In trying to assess whether there is a need for the MLF, the ANF, or some other hardware solution, it is helpful to begin with an unchallenged assertion: From the point of view of American interests, nothing is needed. With the exception of desiring increased conventional forces, the urgency of which has taken a backseat to pressures for the MLF, the United States has not seen any need for change in the security arrangements for the West. United States' officials are confident that the nuclear forces of the Alliance are adequate to deter any form of Soviet aggression and, if there should nevertheless be a war, are adequate to destroy Soviet targets. Thus, for the United States, the MLF is designed to meet the needs and demands of its European allies.

GERMAN INTERESTS

The crux of the Alliance remains the defense of Germany. It was because of a perception of a German demand for control over nuclear weapons that proponents of the MLF pushed the proposal. Because the United States for a time vigorously promoted the MLF, while France actively opposed it, the MLF proposal forced Germany to choose between France and the United States. The Germans were no more pleased by this role than were other members of the Alliance.

While the German interest is often discussed in terms of a share over the control of nuclear weapons, there is a fundamental difference in outlook that separates Germany from the rest of the NATO alliance. Most Europeans are convinced that if there ever was a military threat from the Soviet Union, it has now disappeared with the increase in the West's military and political strength and with the changes in Soviet objectives. Only in Germany does there remain a widespread feeling of insecurity based not only on the exposed position of Berlin but also on the large number of Soviet medium-range missiles trained on Western Europe and the belief that the Soviets could seize much, if not all, of Germany in a surprise attack, should they desire to do so. Thus, for Germany, the main security problem is the Russian threat to Germany. Whether or not they are right, the Germans have become convinced that their territory cannot be successfully defended against any kind of Soviet attack, even a non-nuclear one. They have concluded, therefore, that the attack must be deterred and that it can be prevented only by the certainty of nuclear intervention by the United States. Thus, for German political leaders, the central problem is keeping the United States tied firmly to Europe in general and to Germany in particular. This relationship entails the development of a strategy by the Alliance which publicly states its willingness to employ nuclear weapons early, in the event of conflict. For Germany, then, defense in Europe is to be through deterrence: the deterrent threat of an all-out nuclear war.

The other major German objective, which would have to be dealt with in any long-run plan for the NATO alliance, is the desire to avoid explicit discrimination. Ever since the rearmament of Germany was proposed by the United States early in the 1950's, German political leaders have insisted that if Germany is to take her place as a member of the Western community of nations, it must do so on the basis of complete equality. Thus, it was German insistence on equality within the European Defense Community that led to many changes from the initial proposal accepted in principle by the French National Assembly and that contributed in part to the rejection of EDC by France. Germany is now the only NATO country committed by international treaty not to manufacture nuclear weapons on her own territory; but some German political leaders and many analysts in the United States have argued that in the long-run Germany will be forced to try to acquire a national nuclear capability if the British and French nuclear programs continue.

The MLF is labeled by its proponents as a political device designed to secure cohesion in the Alliance and, in particular, to answer some requests emanating from Germany. However, if Germany's major concerns are of insecurity in Central Europe and long-run discrimination vis-à-vis Britain and France, the MLF does not deal directly with them. It does deal with them indirectly, only if the MLF succeeds in tying the United States closer to Europe. Thus, although German statements on the subject varied and there was some divergence of views, it is evident that German political leaders had no desire to see the elimination of the American veto and the evolvement of the MLF into a European nuclear force. The Germans now believe that if the MLF is desirable, it must serve as a means of linking the United States more intimately with Europe. It must commit American nuclear weapons to the defense of Europe and not provide Europe with a small force at the price of weakening the American involvement. In addition, the Germans realize—and believe the Russians realize —that American nuclear weapons are more likely to be used in their defense than are the relatively smaller forces which would be under the joint control of a group of European governments and whose firing would have to be agreed on by at least some other European powers.

Dispelling the feeling of discrimination in Germany requires not the creation of a new institution but rather the abandonment of national nuclear forces by Britain and France. Thus, the MLF or any other nuclear-sharing arrangement will deal with this problem only if it provides a vehicle for eliminating the British and French nuclear forces.

EUROPEAN INTERESTS

Moving from Germany to the rest of Europe, there is a major distinction between France—or at least the France of Charles de Gaulle—and the other members of the NATO alliance. De Gaulle's desire to create a Europe of nations led by France, independent of the United States, counters all long-run and short-run American objectives. Certainly the MLF was not designed to close the gap between the United States and France; rather, it was designed to highlight the differences, to force the rest of Europe to choose between the United States and France, and to provide a rallying point for those in Europe—particularly the "Europeans" —opposed to de Gaulle. Part of the impetus for pushing the MLF came from the signing of the Franco-German treaty of alliance in 1963 and the feeling that Germany, particularly under Adenauer, might be moving into the Gaullist camp. The initial

German acceptance of the MLF proposal needs also to be understood, at least in part, in light of the feeling that in signing the Franco-German treaty, Germany had perhaps gone too far in appearing to accept de Gaulle's leadership.

Beyond the relationship between France and Germany, the MLF was designed not only to provide a rallying point for anti-Gaullism but also to deal with some existing general European attitudes about the Alliance. There is no fear in the rest of Europe of a Russian military attack; thus, Europeans see no need to change the Alliance in order to improve its military posture vis-à-vis the Soviet Union. There is a vague and long-run fear, capitalized upon by de Gaulle, that the United States might withdraw, leaving Europe naked before Soviet nuclear blackmail. It is doubtful, however, that this view commands any widespread support from the political elite of Europe; apparently the American commitment to Europe has been sufficiently demonstrated.

Another European concern—one which has been, and deserves to be, taken more seriously—is the desire to play a greater role in influencing American policy, particularly on those issues either directly affecting Europe or involving the possible use of nuclear weapons and the risk of an all-out nuclear war. This desire on the part of the Europeans—expressed perhaps most forcefully by British Prime Minister Harold Wilson when he said that Britain did not want control over a small, inefficient force but rather a share in the control of the nuclear force of the Alliance—remains a vague, loosely formulated demand, but one which is acknowledged by all to be real.

Any American policy that seeks to change and strengthen the Atlantic alliance must meet the criteria of maintaining the cohesion of the Alliance as a whole (which means not driving even a Gaullist France completely out of the Alliance) while, at the same time, providing for the possibility of tighter unity with those countries of Europe desiring it. American policy towards Europe must also deal with the explicit German security fears. It must provide procedures that would give Europeans a greater sense of participation in planning for the defense of Europe, especially for the use of nuclear weapons; this means planning for the American strategic nuclear forces and not just for a small force, such as the MLF. Finally, American policy, both because of the long-run problem of the German nuclear force and because of the general interest on the part of the United States in halting the proliferation of nuclear weapons, must be aimed at creating a framework that would furnish a way for Britain and France to phase out their nuclear programs, if they wanted to.

ALTERNATIVE POLICIES

It is in light of the European problems and demands just presented that alternatives—including the MLF, the ANF, and a policy which excludes at least for the moment any hardware solution —need to be evaluated.

As the proponents of the MLF concede, the purpose of the force is political and not military. It is generally agreed that the MLF is neither militarily necessary nor militarily useless. The proposed fleet of surface ships would not be more vulnerable to destruction by the Soviet Union than much of the rest of the nuclear-striking power of the Alliance and would be only somewhat less vulnerable than either Polaris submarines or hardened Minutemen missiles in terms of cost per expected megatonnage which could be delivered to the Soviet Union. Military officials, then, with the exception of some in the British Navy who remain skeptical of the whole idea, tend to be neutral about the proposed MLF; and even American civilians in the Pentagon, including Secretary of Defense Robert S. McNamara, have been on the whole either neutral or uninterested in the MLF arrangement. The creation of the force shows no signs of uniting Europe; but, on the contrary, it is causing disagreements, not only between France and everyone else, but among the other powers.

A major point stressed by the advocates of the MLF is that it must be seen in dynamic terms: it must be flexible and expected to change over time. The question remains, however, will it in fact change and, if so, in what way? There is a major difference in perception of where the MLF should be going. As was indicated above, most Germans see the value of the force as a means of tying the United States more closely with Europe; consequently, they have what might be called an Atlantic image of the MLF. On the other hand, there are some, both in the United States and Europe, who are interested in the creation of a federated

Europe; the MLF, then, would evolve into a European nuclear force under the control of central European institutions. The United States government officially had said that it would consider revising the control procedures for the MLF if a united Europe were in existence. It is difficult to predict whether the MLF is likely to evolve into an Atlantic force or a European force, but it is clear that many of the people now supporting the force will be disillusioned whichever way the evolution goes.

A major difference between the ANF and the MLF is that the ANF would be able to integrate in it British, and perhaps in the long-run French, nuclear forces. By dropping the principle that only multilaterally produced forces could be accepted into the inter-allied force, the ANF could provide the vehicle for enabling Britain and France to phase out their nuclear programs. In this way, Germany's feeling of inequality might largely dissipate.

It seems clear now that if the creation of a NATO nuclear force ever is realized, it will involve a substantial compromise with the ANF proposal. It remains true, however, that any allied nuclear force would exacerbate relations with France, would produce problems in American and European relations with the Soviet Union, would complicate the attempt of the Soviet satellites to increase their independence, and would set back efforts to secure an anti-proliferation agreement with the Soviet Union. Because all of the hardware proposals have proven divisive rather than cohesive, it needs to be asked whether any new force should be created.

The proposal to do nothing in the way of creating new institutions is based on the assumption that because of the increasing aloofness of France and because there is no pressing need on military grounds, the time is not ripe for the creation of an additional nuclear force. Rather, it would appear that the need for the moment is to concentrate on specific problems facing the Alliance and to try to go some distance towards meeting the frequently expressed, but seldom detailed, European desire for an increase in European involvement in the planning on nuclear questions.

It is recognized that a hardware solution would not, in itself, fulfill this European desire; but proponents of a nuclear force frequently state that it will provide the conditions under which the problem can be met. However, whatever can be done with a hardware solution, can be done without it. Giving the Europeans a greater sense of participation can help to dispel any sense of inferiority they may have; in fact, the American government has been taking a number of limited steps in this direction already. Thus, the inter-allied nuclear force was at least arranged at Ottawa; the post of a deputy to the Supreme Allied Commander in Europe for Atomic Affairs was created and has been filled by a Belgian. NATO liaison officers are now at Omaha working with SAC officials to draw up the American integrated strategic nuclear-targeting plan. And in 1965, on American initiative, a special committee was set up to improve coordination on nuclear issues. In addition, since 1960 there has been a great increase in the sharing of information on American nuclear strategy between the United States and Europe.

In seeking to increase the European role, it is necessary to begin with a fundamental fact, which is perhaps better understood in Europe than it is in some places in the United States: One man— and one man alone—must make the decision to use nuclear weapons. European security, in addition to American security, would be diluted if the President of the United States were forced to share with any person or committee the power to launch nuclear war. Thus, influence can be brought to bear not on the final agonizing decision but rather on planning for the size of the force, the options which the force is given, and the actions which should be taken before the use of nuclear weapons is contemplated. Planning not only limits what can be done but can create new opportunities and new options for the use of military force. It is in this area that further steps might be taken.

Such steps would include turning the working groups of the select committee into organs of real consultation. Working meetings of officials at the assistant-secretary level might be initiated along the lines of the Organization for Economic Cooperation and Development (OECD) operations. Perhaps, most important, European governments, particularly Britain and Germany, should be encouraged to advance concrete proposals.

If, by insisting that the Europeans come up with an agreed plan before anything is done, the MLF and related plans are allowed to die, the immediate gains would be cohesion and the opening-up of opportunities both to improve relations with Eastern Europe and to halt the spread of nuclear weapons. As far as NATO itself is concerned, it is generally agreed that there are no urgent problems that need to be dealt with nor that could be alleviated by a hardware solution.

SELECTED BIBLIOGRAPHY

Bowie, Robert R. *Shaping the Future*. New York: Columbia University Press, 1964.
Buchan, Alastair, and Philip Windsor. *Arms and Stability in Europe*. London: Chatto & Windus, 1963.
Kissinger, Henry A. *The Troubled Partnership*. New York: McGraw-Hill Book Co., 1965.
Osgood, Robert E. *NATO, The Entangling Alliance*. Chicago: University of Chicago Press, 1962.

CHAPTER ELEVEN

Deterrence and Defense in Asia

If a predominance of nuclear weapons could provide for a country the ability to control all events with which it was concerned, then the United States would be in complete control of the Asian situation. An examination of the current nuclear balance of power in Asia reveals an overwhelming preponderance of American power, which is not offset—as it was for a time in Europe—by a preponderant conventional capability of the opposing side. Yet American influence is clearly limited.

In attempting to outline the nature and size of American nuclear forces in the Pacific, it is necessary to begin with two caveats. First, these forces appear to be growing in size in response to the Chinese nuclear detonations and the crisis in Vietnam. Secondly, because the United States has very substantial nuclear forces that can be moved into the Pacific area on very short notice, it is necessary to take into account the American strategic and nuclear forces based in the United States.

The United States is known to have land-based nuclear forces in the Pacific area, but their exact locations have not been publicly announced. There are B-52's stationed in Guam and fighters and short-range missiles capable of firing nuclear weapons on Taiwan, Okinawa, and Korea.

The American sea-based nuclear force has been growing in size. The United States now has two Polaris submarines stationed in the Pacific and has plans for two more in the near future. In addition, the planes of the Seventh Fleet presumably have a nuclear, as well as a conventional, capability.

Much less is known publicly about the nature of the Soviet forces in the Far East. The Soviets apparently have some of their very large number of medium- and intermediate-range missile force in the Far East. These missiles, at least initially, were intended to be used against Japan and American bases. The Soviets also have a limited long-range bomber force that very unlikely would be used in the Far East. In addition, the Soviet intercontinental missile force and limited submarine-launched missile force could presumably be brought to bear in the Far East. Soviet missiles appear to have longer range than the American five thousand-mile missiles, and these missiles could be targeted towards the Far East. However, the extent to which they are currently targeted towards the Far East or could be quickly changed in their target pattern is not known.

The question of how to treat the aggregate of Soviet and Chinese nuclear capability in the Pacific is an obscure one; some of the facets of this problem will be treated later on. At this point it need only be stated that the Soviet force might well be targeted against China, as well as in support of Chinese forces. It is interesting to note that to the arrival of an American nuclear submarine in Japan, to the stationing of American Polaris submarines in the Pacific, and to the American assertion that it might establish a base in the Indian Ocean, both the Soviet Union and Communist China reacted in terms of their own security. The Russians have pointed out that these actions increased Russian insecurity and the danger of American encirclement of the Soviet Union, while the Chinese talked about the increased American capability against China. In the propaganda of the two countries, neither has alluded to the growing danger to the other nor to the possibility of combined action to confront this danger.

A Chinese nuclear force appears at the present time (1966) to be, for all effective purposes, non-existent. While the Chinese may well be stockpiling some material in excess of what they are using in their bomb-test series, it appears extremely doubtful that they as yet have an operational bomb. However, the Chinese may well be expected to have, at some time in the near future, a twenty-kiloton or larger weapon deliverable in the bomber aircraft they now have.

Turning to the future of the Asian nuclear balance, the uncertainty becomes even greater. It appears likely that the American nuclear force will stabilize at approximately the current levels with the probable exception of the assignment of several additional Polaris submarines to the Pacific Fleet, as these become available. As the Chinese nuclear force grows in size, pressures may develop to reduce the vulnerabilities of the American theater-based forces in the Pacific. Presumably forces that were put in when the Chinese were lacking any nuclear capability will need to be altered in light of the growing Chinese nuclear threat. However, the Chinese counter-force attack against American theater-based forces appears for a variety of reasons to be among the least likely contingencies, and it is doubtful whether large funds should be appropriated for the development of hard and dispersed nuclear forces in the Pacific theater.

The Soviet forces are unlikely to undergo any major change, unless the Soviets should decide that their relation with the Chinese has reached a point where they need to install a very substantial MRBM capability directed specifically at China. Whether such a development will in fact occur is impossible to determine, given the volatile nature of the Sino-Soviet relationship.

The size and shape of a Chinese force over the next decade or two is very uncertain. Possibly its evolution will be the most significant change in the Asian nuclear balance. The major Chinese commitment to the development of a nuclear capability, which has brought them as far as they have gotten at present, makes it evident (as was indicated in Chapter Six) that Peking assigns a high priority to the goal of becoming a militarily effective nuclear power.

The Chinese desire for great-power status and for a capability to deter a United States attack—both of which would leave the Chinese free to establish their hegemony in Asia—leads them to seek a strategic deterrent capability. The Chinese have denigrated the role of tactical nuclear weapons; and it appears that, in fact, they will not try to develop any kind of arsenal of nuclear weapons to be used in ground military action. Both for deterrence of an American attack and for advancement of their status as a great power—the leading power of Asia—the Chinese will almost certainly concentrate on "modern" strategic systems designed to demonstrate their nuclear parity with the major nuclear powers. For this reason and because of their lack of aircraft, it is likely that the Chinese will concentrate on a missile force mated with thermonuclear warheads. The Chinese desire to keep the cost of the program as low as possible, so as not to disrupt any more than necessary their industrial development, suggests that the Chinese will concentrate on a very few systems—perhaps as few as one medium-range missile and, less certainly, one intercontinental missile system. The form of the intercontinental system, whether it be an ICBM or a submarine-launched missile, is probably not yet settled in Peking; and it may be that the Chinese, at least in the short run, will focus on medium-range missiles in their effort to deter the United States.

In the late 1960's the Chinese will be able to deploy a deliverable multi-stage weapon that could be mated with an operational MRBM. This development will mark a major change in the Pacific nuclear balance of power. From that time forward, the United States—and perhaps the Soviet Union—will have to deal with a country with the capability to kill millions of Asians within a very few minutes. The Chinese MRBM force is likely to grow over the 1970's and to reach a size of over one hundred missiles by the mid-to-late 1970's. A further change will occur when the Chinese develop the capability to threaten land missiles on the territory of the United States. This could happen perhaps as early as 1975 and will almost certainly occur within the 1980's. The Chinese intercontinental capability could take the form of submarine-launched missiles or ICBM's based in China. The size and shape of such a force is probably not clearly determined, even in Peking. It is thought that all of the Chinese nuclear forces will be extremely vulnerable to an American first strike.

A final uncertainty about the nature of the Pacific nuclear situation in the coming decades involves the question of whether additional Asian powers will decide to develop their own nuclear forces or will begin to receive nuclear weapons from nuclear powers. Among the countries which might fall into one or both of these categories are India, Japan, Australia, and perhaps Indonesia. It now appears likely that the Indian government will, sometime over the next decade, decide to produce an independent Indian nuclear force. Such a force is likely to consist, at least initially, of only twenty-kiloton fission weapons that will be delivered in current or to-be-procured foreign aircraft. However, the presence of such a force will complicate the existing nuclear balance. A Japanese nuclear force could have a much greater impact on the Asian nuclear situation, but the likelihood of Japan developing such a force remains highly problematical. Japan could, without any great effect on its growth rate, develop a nuclear capability far in excess of that of the Chinese. It should be noted, for example, that the Japanese have a very advanced missile program—one which could easily be used in a developing nuclear program. For other countries in the area, the possibility of becoming a nuclear power would appear to depend on assistance from current nuclear powers, although the fact that Australia could develop its own nuclear force sometime in the 1970's is not to be overlooked. Finally, if the Indonesians were to develop a nuclear force, they would probably be dependent on substantial assistance, either from the Soviet Union or Communist China.

Thus, by the mid-1970's the Pacific nuclear balance is likely to be perceptibly transformed from what it is at present. American force, might well have been developed. Even more important, Chinese forces will have grown to the point where, although they will be vulnerable, they will give China an operational capability, at least in the Asian theater. Russian forces will probably remain at current levels, although there may be a substantial increase to counter the Chinese. Other nuclear forces, particularly an Indian force, might well have been developed. However, perhaps paradoxically, the role of nuclear deterrents in Asia may not have changed appreciably because of these developments.

We now turn to the current and the future role of American nuclear weapons in deterring aggression in Asia. The role of any weapons systems in deterrence must be considered in relation to both the countries, or groups, against which the deterrent threat is directed and the actions of that group which are to be deterred. The image of the United States confronting a monolithic Communist bloc consisting of the Soviet Union, China, small Communist states in Asia and Europe, as well as Communist parties united and taking direction from a single leader in Moscow, has been effectively shattered by the events of the last five years or more. It is now clear that the United States confronts a variety of different Communist threats. This is not to say that the Communist states might not align with each other in certain situations and under certain pressures from the United States or that they might not even coordinate some offensive actions. Rather, it is to suggest that a credible threat against one center of Communist power— for example, Moscow—may no longer be sufficient—assuming that it ever was—to deter actions by Peking, not to speak of those of North Vietnam or the Indonesian Communist party. Thus, in seeking to assess the role of deterrence in Asia, we must distinguish between deterrent threats directed at the Soviet Union, those directed at Communist China, those directed at other Communist parties in power (North Vietnam and North Korea), and those directed at Communist insurgency groups or political parties in countries such as Indonesia or South Vietnam. It is obvious that the problems in each case will be different. A threat to bomb Hanoi, for example, may look much less threatening to China than to the North Vietnamese and perhaps even less threatening to Moscow. On the other hand, threats of massive retaliation directed against the Soviet homeland may appear unreal, incredible, and not operative for local Communist forces.

All of the possible sources of violence and aggression in Asia do not stem from communism. The United States is also interested in deterring military action between various states in Asia, including India, Pakistan, Malaysia, Indonesia, South Vietnam, and Cambodia. In none of these cases has the United States sought thus far to bring into play its nuclear-deterrent capability.

In determining the situations in which deterrent threats may be effective, the second factor to be considered is what actions are to be deterred. In the Asian theater, violence has taken a great variety of forms ranging from rioting and political assassination through wars of national liberation to conventional wars. In addition, the United States has sought to deter the possibility of the expansion of a conventional war to the use of nuclear weapons. Finally, as the military power of China grows, the United States will want to be in a position to counter the political effect of Chinese threats of nuclear blackmail, as it has already dealt with Soviet threats.

As has already been indicated, a pairing-off of the various kinds of actions with the countries or groups being deterred provides a wide range of possibilities. However, for most of these, nuclear deterrence has not been used and appears to be irrelevant. For some, such as a Soviet nuclear attack on Japan, the efficacy of nuclear deterrence seems obvious enough so that a separate treatment is not necessary. The most important problems will occur in relation to the deterrence of Communist China, from actions ranging from support for wars of national liberation through conventional war and various efforts to exploit China's growing nuclear capability. The remainder of the chapter will therefore focus on the role of American nuclear and conventional power in deterring or defending against such Chinese actions.

In discussing the European situation, it is often said that there is no way of telling if deterrence works, since it is not known whether the Soviet Union has in effect contemplated military action. Others would turn around and assert that clearly deterrence has worked, because there has been no military action. Either way this problem is approached, deterrence has not "worked" in Asia. Despite the vast preponderance of American power, which has been even greater in earlier periods, the Communist-bloc countries have engaged in a number of acts of military violence across international boundaries in the Far East. There are, then, a series of actions that have been taken in the past and might be taken in the future by Communist groups in Asia, particularly by Communist China, which might be called "undeterrable" actions; that is, actions that fall below any ability of the United States to effectively bring its nuclear power to bear.

Thus far in the postwar period, Chinese undeterrable actions have fallen into four categories:

1. *Conventional military action.* This has occurred beyond what the Chinese claim to be their international borders only once, at the time of the Chinese intervention in the Korean War. Even at the time of the intervention the Chinese were influenced by American atomic power. There have been no signs of even a threat of this kind of conventional intervention by the Chinese since 1950;

and it appears that such action will continue to be deterred and is, in fact, now in the "overdeterred" category (discussed below).

2. *Conventional military action within "Chinese territory."* The major military adventure by the Chinese Communists in the post-war period was the invasion of Tibet in 1950. This has been followed by continuous effort to suppress Tibetan revolts. Chinese action here was taken with the notion that Tibet was indisputably a part of China. The reaction of the United States to the event, including the failure to ask for General Assembly condemnation, indicated that the United States took a similar view of the Tibetan action. The Chinese now have a completely free hand in running Tibet and are continuing to suppress the minor Tibetan attempts to throw the Chinese out. It seems unlikely that any American nuclear or conventional power would be brought to bear in this kind of situation.

3. *Border probes.* Chinese probes around their borders have been concentrated mainly against India and in the Taiwan Straits against the offshore islands, which the Chinese consider to be part of their own territory. In these cases the action has been very limited and of relatively short duration. To some extent, action has been explicitly designed to fall below the American nuclear threshold—has been sufficiently limited so that the United States would not respond with nuclear weapons.

These events are "undeterrable" only in the sense that the Chinese can always find some low-level military pressure that will be below the threshold of nuclear deterrence. However, how much probing they could expect to get away with, without running the risk of provoking American nuclear threats, can only be surmised.

4. *Support for wars of national liberation.* The major Chinese action here has been in support of actions in the Indochinese Peninsula. Here again the degree of support rendered by the Chinese could be affected by nuclear threats, but it seems likely that there would remain a degree of activity which would not run any risk of bringing on a nuclear attack against China. The basic Chinese position is that foreign governments can lend only moral support, train guerrillas, and give limited military aid. These actions appear unlikely to provoke an American nuclear attack.

At the other end of the spectrum, there are a series of situations that appear to be "overdeterred": as in Europe, there are an abundance of political and military incentives working against aggression. Where Europe and Asia differ in this regard, however, is in the conventional capabilities of the opposing sides. At times in the postwar period—whether or not it still is true—the Soviet Union did have conventional superiority in Europe. Such superiority on the part of the Communist bloc in Asia existed, if at all, only in the early months of 1950, when the American Army remained almost entirely a potential military force. There is no doubt now, however, that in the 1960's and for the foreseeable future American conventional military power is sufficient to defeat and, consequently, to deter a Chinese Communist effort to invade any of the islands off the mainland of Asia—among others, Japan, Taiwan, and beyond to the Philippines, Malaysia, and Indonesia. American conventional power also appears to be adequate to defeat and to deter a Chinese attempt to invade India or to re-invade South Korea. It is very difficult to assess the role that nuclear deterrence plays in these situations. American nuclear power is probably sufficient by itself to prevent a Chinese Communist attack against Japan, India, Taiwan, Malaysia, etc., while, on the other hand, American conventional power alone is sufficient to deter these actions. Finally, it remains uncertain whether, even barring American conventional and nuclear capability, the Chinese would have been tempted to undertake military moves, except against Taiwan. More positively we can say: As long as the United States has any nuclear force, it will play a role in deterring Chinese military moves; but the United States could depend, both in its planning and in its deterrent statements, on the threat of a conventional response.

The "deterred" is what lies in between the "undeterrable" and the "overdeterred"; that is, those actions which Communist China might well have contemplated in the postwar period but which were deterred by American nuclear capability. No attempt can be made to be exhaustive about this category, since we are dealing with what is essentially unknown—unknown perhaps even to Peking. The Communists came to power in China after the United States had developed nuclear weapons; consequently, they have always had to assess their foreign policy opportunities in relation to American superiority in nuclear weapons. There may be certain tactics and certain objectives that have never come to the fore, but that might have if the United States had not possessed a nuclear capability or had not seemed willing to use it under certain circumstances in Asia.

Chinese Communist moves in the Taiwan Straits, particularly against the offshore islands of Quemoy and Matsu, appear to fall within the category of deterred actions. It is difficult to make any general assessment of the possibility of conventional defense of the offshore islands. However, given the relative neglect of American conventional capability in the late 1950's, it seems possible that there were at least some periods of time during which Quemoy could have been captured in spite of an American and Chinese Nationalist conventional defense. In any event, Peking might have tried further moves against the offshore islands, in the absence of an American nuclear capability. It is also possible, but by no means certain, that further moves against India might have taken place in the absence of an American nuclear capability.

The Chinese might also have been willing to increase their involvement in particular local conflicts if the American nuclear threat had not been present. They might have fought longer in Korea, they might have pressed further during the 1958 Quemoy crisis, and they might well at the moment be giving increased aid to North Vietnam were it not for the fear of an American nuclear attack against China.

It is argued, then, that there are some events in the middle range, where American nuclear power may play a critical role, although this middle range is difficult to specify in the abstract. Nevertheless, it is felt that this range is bounded on the one side by actions which we have not at any time been able to deter and, on the other, by actions which seem overdeterred.

As was indicated in Chapter Six, the Chinese are developing a nuclear capability at least partly in order to be in a position in which they can deter more effectively an American nuclear attack. However, as President Johnson pointed out in a public statement, later picked up and attacked in Peking: Chinese testing can only "increase the insecurity of the Chinese people." In fact—and the Chinese appear to recognize this fact—the United States may be more likely to use nuclear weapons against China now that China has begun to develop her own nuclear capability; in this situation, the United States would be using nuclear weapons against a nuclear power which, at least implicitly, was threatening to use her own nuclear weapons in the area of local conflict. In addition, Chinese nuclear installations provide an obvious target for a limited American nuclear attack. Thus, in the current period, the Chinese may be expected to be even more cautious; and the range of deterrable actions may extend even further.

As the Chinese develop a nuclear-delivery capability directed initially at Asian cities, their confidence in their ability to deter American intervention is likely to increase. It will increase even further when they have the ability to attack the United States. The Chinese may then be willing to probe the limits of the undeterrable; that is, they may increase their support of wars of national liberation in the Asian area and may begin to probe along their own borders, perhaps again in the Taiwan Straits.

As Chinese nuclear power grows, the United States may find itself more cautious. On the strategic level, the President and his advisers will be confronted with the realization that in any Asian crisis they will be up against a nuclear power capable of wreaking great nuclear destruction in Asia and at least limited nuclear destruction on the United States. This fact would appear to provide some pressure against greater American involvement in Asian crises, although, of course, it is not a total determinant of what American policy would be. The development of the Chinese nuclear capability may impose on the United States some tactical caution as well. For example, the United States might be reluctant to concentrate its troops in a few places, as it appears now to be doing in Vietnam, when the Chinese have a nuclear force that could destroy these concentrated installations very quickly. While there are a number of reasons to believe that China would never use her nuclear weapons in this way, the existence of this capability would almost certainly have some effect on American deployment.

Perhaps more important, other countries in Asia may become less confident of American willingness to use nuclear weapons in their defense and less willing to accept the use of American nuclear weapons in a situation in which a nuclear war may be reciprocal.

The already limited usefulness of American nuclear power in

Asia may thus be further eroded as China develops her own nuclear capability; this fact must be considered by the United States in assessing what is likely to be an efficacious policy in the 1970's and 1980's.

The United States currently faces a problem similar to the one it faced in Europe in the early Eisenhower Administration; it will be important for the United States to avoid the European "syndrome," which has contributed to the current crisis on NATO defense policy. In Asia, now, the United States has virtual unilateral possession of nuclear weapons, which it had in Europe in the early 1950's. As a result, there is a tendency on the part of the United States, which existed in relation to Europe as well, to rely on nuclear weapons, including tactical nuclear weapons, to make up for the manpower and conventional-weapons advantage of its opponent. In such a situation, the value of tactical nuclear weapons and the adequacy and necessity of nuclear weapons to deter or to defend against aggression is overplayed. This may well lead to pressure for nuclear-base arrangements and for the stationing of American nuclear weapons on Asian territory. Another outgrowth of this situation is a general indifference to, or in some cases opposition to, the buildup of indigenous conventional capability, on the grounds that it is at best superfluous and economically wasteful in a period in which economic growth is a critical variable. There is also a tendency to consider and possibly to begin the implementation of programs of nuclear assistance designed to create independent national nuclear powers, or regional or alliance nuclear forces. All of these phenomena characterized the American policy towards Europe in the mid-1950's and are beginning to characterize American policy towards Asia in the mid-to-late 1960's.

The effect of America's policy towards Europe in the mid-1950's on current American doctrines and attitudes in Europe should provide some warning of the danger of repeating this process in the Far East. The results may well be the same. The emphasis on the adequacy and effectiveness of nuclear deterrence can only serve to cast doubt on the credibility and effectiveness of United States' conventional forces, especially as the credibility of the American nuclear deterrent declines with the growth of Chinese nuclear power. The obvious results would be pressure for independent national nuclear forces and a weakening of the desire for, and the belief in, the efficacy of both indigenous and American conventional defense efforts.

These dangers can be avoided now by stressing the value and role of conventional forces—both American and local—by noting that China can be—and is—deterred by conventional forces in most, if not all, areas surrounding her borders. American statements should convey the fact that China can be defeated in any conventional war beyond her own borders. Finally, it should be clear—and should be made clear—that nuclear weapons do play a role—primarily a deterring role—against any use of nuclear weapons by China. The United States has every reason to assert that it would not hesitate to respond with American nuclear forces to a launching of nuclear weapons by the Chinese. In dealing with lower levels of aggression, American nuclear forces are already of limited value; their limitations are likely to grow as Chinese nuclear capability increases. American nuclear power will continue to be a vital element in defending the Far East; but it is not now, nor will it be in the future, a substitute for conventional force.

SELECTED BIBLIOGRAPHY

Barnett, A. Doak. *Communist China and Asia.* New York: Harper, 1960.
Buchan, Alastair, ed. *China and the Peace of Asia.* New York: Frederick A. Praeger, 1965.
Jordon, Amos. *Foreign Aid and the Security of Southeast Asia.* New York: Frederick A. Praeger, 1962.
Kennedy, D. E. *The Security of Southern Asia.* London: Chatto & Windus, 1965.

CHAPTER TWELVE

Counter-insurgency:
The Challenge of
Revolutionary War

The use of force to bring about a change in the political leadership and form of government is a common characteristic of the political scene in most of the countries in the world, in particular, the countries of Africa, Asia, and Latin America. The kinds of violence range from relatively peaceful and bloodless coups d'état to major civil war. The causes of the use of violence are equally varied. They range from essentially domestic issues, such as the dissatisfaction of military leaders about corruption within the civil government, through international considerations, including the political orientation of the country involved. Support from the outside frequently plays a critical role in attempts to overthrow governments violently; such support may come from a variety of sources and countries including various Communist governments and organizations.

We will be concerned in this chapter with only one aspect of the most effective American strategy for coming to grips with political change in the third world—including violent change— either implemented by a domestic Communist party or supported by the Soviet Union or Communist China. We seek, then, to develop an effective strategy for, what is known as, *counter-insurgency* in dealing with, what the Soviet Union and China call, *wars of national liberation.*

THE SINO-SOVIET DISPUTE AND WARS OF NATIONAL LIBERATION

Both the Soviet Union and Communist China view wars of national liberation as a desirable means of effecting change in underdeveloped areas and of eventually establishing Communist governments. Their joint position was stated in the Moscow Statement of 1960. In that document both countries—in fact, all the Communist parties of the world—argued that revolutionary wars were "just wars" which needed support and which were desirable in order to bring about the establishment of Communist regimes. The differences between Communist China and the Soviet Union lie primarily in their interpretations of this basic document; these differences have been exaggerated, not only by observers, but also in the polemics issued by the Communist parties of China and the Soviet Union. However, general differences do exist, as stated in the polemics. The Soviet Union tends to be more moderate in its support for wars of national liberation and in its suggestions that alternative roads to power for Communist parties, including peaceful transition, are possible. The Chinese, on the other hand, urge greater support for wars of national liberation and have probably contributed a greater percentage of their relatively limited resources towards promoting revolution than has the Soviet Union. The proper strategy for wars of national liberation has been a much-discussed issue between the Soviet Union and Communist China, with the Chinese pressing the Russians to take a more vigorous stand in providing material and diplomatic support for revolutionary movements.

Why has the Soviet position been one of greater moderation? Perhaps the basic reason is that the Soviet leadership has much less confidence in the success of wars of national liberation. The Soviet Communist party came to power in a relatively bloodless coup rather than a long military struggle. Moreover, since then the Soviet Union has helped to put in power a number of Communist parties, particularly in Eastern Europe, which have come to power again without a major guerrilla war. The current Soviet leadership is divorced from guerrilla struggle and does not view it as a decidedly effective or necessary means of bringing about social change or a Communist state.

Another factor is that Soviet leaders may have greater confidence that the world will move in directions favorable to them without employing violence within particular countries. The Soviet Union has the economic and political capability to survive in a world that remains non-Communist for a long time; it also has the economic and military means to influence the world in the directions it wishes it to go, without interfering in certain countries and devoting a major effort to stimulating revolutionary war. In addition, the areas in which the Soviet Union would most like to have success in spreading its influence and instituting Communist governments is in Europe, specifically, Central Europe. The European theater continues to be the prime center of Soviet foreign-policy interests. This difference in perspective has a major impact on the general nature of the Sino-Soviet dispute and, in particular, affects the extent to which the two countries see revolutionary war as a primary means for accomplishing the spread of communism. For controlling political developments in Central Europe, revolutionary war does not appear to be a very useful tool; for influencing the third world, however, guerrilla warfare will more likely be effective.

A question which probably receives more consideration in Moscow than it does in Peking is that of the relationship between support for revolutionary wars and the danger of general nuclear war. As has been stated before, the Chinese desire to avoid general nuclear war no less than the Soviet Union or the United States does. However, the Chinese probably have a greater feeling of confidence that the United States will not launch general nuclear war in retaliation for support given to wars of national liberation. They feel this way because of a somewhat greater propensity on their part to run risks and to downgrade the likelihood of an American response, perhaps coupled with some less complete awareness of the real nature of the strategic balance and the relative weakness of the Soviet Union. Most important, the Chinese have a different estimate of the will and determination of the United States. The Soviet Union has seen the United States go to the brink of nuclear war in resisting challenges to the American position in Cuba and Berlin in a way that no American counterpart in the Far East has. In fact, in its conduct in the Taiwan Straits, Korea, and elsewhere in the Far East, the United States has appeared to be unwilling to move as close to general nuclear war as it has been vis-à-vis the Soviet Union. As a result, the Chinese have a different perspective of the likely danger of a guerrilla war turning into a general nuclear war.

This brief discussion suggests why there are differences between Soviet and Chinese policy; but, before turning to a more detailed consideration of the Chinese strategy of revolutionary war, it is worth noting that the similarities probably overshadow these differences. Both countries support wars of national liberation; both are prepared to aid them and have aided particular revolutionary movements. The differences, as has been suggested, involve specific kinds of support for specific countries.

CHINESE POLICY

The current leadership of Communist China spent most of its life engaged in revolutionary warfare. The Communist party came to power in China after prolonged and bitter civil war. It started out as a very small group and increased its power and strength until ultimately it was able to defeat the Chinese Nationalists and establish effective control through all of China. It is not surprising, given this background, that the leaders in Peking view revolutionary warfare as the most effective means of spreading Communist and Chinese influence throughout the world. Experiences in Vietnam, Cuba, and Algeria have tended to reinforce the view that revolutionary war could be successful and could lead to the ascendancy of a Communist regime.

In 1949 the Chinese Communists began to elaborate their own doctrine of revolutionary warfare based explicitly on the Chinese Communist route to power. This doctrine advocated, essentially, relying on the peasants to establish a firm mass base in the countryside. This power in the countryside was to be used ultimately to surround and attack the cities in order to setup Communist rule throughout the country.

The role that the Communist party has had to play in this

process has varied from time to time in Chinese Communist ideological literature. In the period immediately following 1949, the assumption was that a Communist party would have to lead the revolution, which would be, in effect, two revolutions in one— overthrowing imperialism and capitalism at the same time and establishing a Communist regime. During the mid-to-late 1950's and into the 1960's, the Chinese model assumed that a nationalist revolution could precede the Communist revolution. Thus, the Chinese held that support should be given to nationalist groups, such as the Algerian liberation front, which was seeking to overthrow imperialist control. It was believed that this first revolution would pave the way for a takeover by a Communist party. However, in mid-1965, with setbacks in Algeria and Indonesia, the Chinese began to reemphasize the pure Chinese Communist model of revolutionary war: a peasant base with an army under the control of a Communist party. Moreover, they talked again of their world view: that the underdeveloped areas were, in effect, the "countryside" of the world; the capitalist states, the "cities," which would be ultimately undermined after the revolution in the underdeveloped areas. In all its variations, the Chinese doctrine of revolutionary war has stressed that peaceful change is impossible. It has pointed both to the danger of attempting to work within the parliamentary system and to the need of securing a firm base in rural areas and of winning the support of the people.

Another reason for attaching so much importance to revolutionary war in Chinese Communist ideology is the limited economic and political power of China, which forces the leaders in Peking to rely on guerrilla war. The Chinese can afford to export the necessary items for fighting a revolutionary war. In contrast to the aid which is necessary to support a major conventional war, what is needed in a war of national liberation is limited supplies of arms, aid in the training of cadres and troops, and training manuals. Therefore, by and large, what revolutionaries need, the Chinese can supply. Until the United States began to bomb North Vietnam, the Chinese could provide everything that the North Vietnamese needed to carry out the revolution in the south. In areas further away from China, in Africa and Latin America, the Chinese capability to supply even limited quantities of arms is not very great, but what they can supply can be of critical importance in these countries. The export of revolution, then, is cheap; and to China, with its limited economic resources, this can be very important.

In addition, the Chinese hold that the right local conditions in a country are a prerequisite for revolutionary war. They do not believe that revolution can be exported at any time and into any country. Local conditions are thought to be the major factor, and outside aid can be only of limited value in wars of national liberation.

With the exception of the Indochinese Peninsula, the Chinese interest in wars of national liberation has been greater for a particular country, the farther that country is from the Chinese border. In these areas, support for revolutionary war is the only means that the Chinese have of influencing events and of setting up a regime which would be friendly to them. Around the Chinese border, the Chinese prefer to rely on the use of military pressure of a traditional sort to increase their control and bring into power governments favorable to them.

AMERICAN POLICY

The United States is now confronted in Vietnam, and will undoubtedly be confronted in the future, with attempts by local Communist groups, aided by either the Soviet Union or Communist China or both, to capture control of a country by the use of violence. As long as the United States seeks to prevent the spread of areas under the control of Communist parties and influenced by Peking or Moscow, it will need to develop a strategy to deal with this threat.

Particularly since 1961, with the growing attention in the United States to the problem of counter-insurgency, it has become a cliché to say that the problem is mainly political rather than military. It is both a military and a political problem; although, if it is confused with the term "ideological," the use of the term "political" may be misleading. By the ideological problem we mean finding and presenting an alternative to communism that will appeal to the people in underdeveloped areas. The political issue, however, is providing the people with a government whose goods and services they see as more desirable than that presented to them by the alternative Communist government. People, in general, tend to be motivated, not by commitment to abstract ideologies, but by perception of their own short-run economic and security interests.

In attempting to enunciate some general principles of American policy for counter-insurgency, it is necessary to begin by underlining what was stated about limited war: local conditions and local issues may supersede any general principles that are established. The way in which insurgency is prevented or defeated in Vietnam will be very different from the way it is handled in the countries of Latin America or Africa. In a sense, one needs a different counter-insurgency policy for each area in which the threat of counter-insurgency looms, perhaps for each country or part of a country in which the threat arises. Nevertheless, a few general points can be made.

In classic Maoist doctrine, the revolutionary war passes through three stages. In the first stage, guerrillas undertake to harrass the government. In the second stage, the guerrillas hold some areas and engage in some coordinated forms of military activity but avoid major combat. In the third stage, a revolutionary government may be established and the guerrillas engage in something approaching regular military combat. Different strategies are needed to cope with the three stages of the revolutionary war.

The first effort, and the one that has by and large been successful, is the prevention of any major guerrilla activities; that is, elimination of the first stage. Communists have attempted to start revolutionary wars in a number of countries—for example, in Thailand—and have thus far been unsuccessful. Seeking to stop the revolt at the first stage is mainly a political endeavor; the providing of goods and services rather than providing an alternative coherent ideology should be emphasized. It is important to establish a sense of loyalty to the central government and a feeling in the people that the central government is satisfying the grievances of the people. It is the struggle at this level that is now going on in Thailand and in a number of countries in Latin America.

If the effort to prevent the first stage from beginning fails, coping with overt military action, presumably increasing in magnitude and intensity and leading ultimately to a stage in which regular military units are being used, becomes the next difficulty. In dealing with these issues, the problem is, at least in significant part, a military one. The introduction of a large number of American military forces in Vietnam in 1965, for example, substantially reduced the possibility that the Saigon government would be overthrown and a Communist regime established in all of Vietnam. At this stage, the quality of the military forces is as important as their support by the people. The United States, with its vastly superior logistics capability, its heavier firepower, and its ability to use air power, has been able to prevent any large-scale Vietcong victories, regardless of the loyalties of the people.

The events in Vietnam also illustrate the fact that most people tend to be motivated, not by abstract appeals, but rather by their perception of the course of action that is most likely to lead to their own personal security and to the satisfaction of their economic, social, and psychological desires. Thus, for example, large-scale American bombing in South Vietnam may have antagonized a number of people; but, at the same time, it demonstrated to these people that the Vietcong could not guarantee their security as it had been able to do before the bombing and that the belief in an imminent victory for the Vietcong might turn out to be dangerously false.

However, even if preponderant military strength can prevent the success of the third stage and can perhaps shift the operations of the guerrillas to the second or first stage, it cannot succeed by itself in wiping out the guerrilla forces and reducing the revolution to the level of nuisance and banditry. The skills that were originally successful in preventing large-scale guerrilla activity need to be applied again; and, implicit in this, are the problems of nation building and political development—areas far beyond the scope of this study.

SELECTED BIBLIOGRAPHY

Black, Cyril E., and Thomas P. Thornton, eds. *Communism and Revolution.* Princeton, N.J.: Princeton University Press, 1964.

Galula, David. *Counter-insurgency Warfare.* New York: Frederick A. Praeger, 1964.

Mao Tse-tung. *Selected Military Writings.* Peking: Foreign Languages Press, 1963.

Thompson, Sir Robert. *Defeating Communist Insurgency: Experiences from Malaya and Vietnam.* Institute for Strategic Studies, Studies in International Security, No. 10. London and New York: Chatto & Windus and Frederick A. Praeger, 1966.

CHAPTER THIRTEEN

Arms Control:
Approaches and Issues

The desire "to turn swords into plowshares" has been part of the dream of mankind since the creation of the first organized military force. Thinking about the possibilities for control over military forces has traditionally been viewed as antithetical to the study of military strategy and the role of force in international politics. It is only within the past decade, with the advent of weapons of great destructive power, that students of military strategy have begun to consider the role that formal, or perhaps tacit, arrangements with potential enemies might play in securing the objectives for which military forces are created. At the same time, at least some advocates of disarmament have recognized the need to consider the strategic, technological aspects of weapons systems in designing proposals for arms control and disarmament. There has thus emerged a new approach to problems of arms control and disarmament—an approach that views efforts either to negotiate formal agreements between countries or to arrive at tacit understandings which restrain or channel the arms race as part of the general effort to use military force to secure the political purposes of the nation. Advocates of arms control tend to emphasize the cooperative aspects of the adversary relationship, even between potential enemies. They point in particular to the desire of all nations to avoid a nuclear war.

There have been differences in opinion among various students of arms control and disarmament. There has been conflict, for example, over the relative importance attached to the political, as opposed to the strategic or military, implications of arms-control agreements. Perhaps the most fundamental conflict has been over the ultimate goal of arms control.

Some advocates of arms control have seen various kinds of formal and informal arrangements between the United States and the Soviet Union as leading ultimately to general and complete disarmament (GCD); that is, the total elimination of organized international military forces except for a force under the control of the United Nations or some similar international institution. Others have seen arms control as being aimed at producing a system of stabilized deterrence under which the United States and the Soviet Union would continue to have relatively small nuclear forces and in which the strategic arms race would be brought to a halt. Still others have viewed arms-control agreements as not having a particular end of their own but rather as being one means to seek international and national security for the United States and other countries. Arms control, then, would be one tool, along with unilateral military actions, diplomacy, and others, that would function as part of a never-ending process to reduce the likelihood of war and increase the security of the United States and its allies, along with the Soviet Union and perhaps China.

In 1959, Soviet Premier Nikita Khrushchev, in a speech to the United Nations General Assembly, proposed that primary attention in disarmament negotiations be given to writing a treaty for general and complete disarmament. The United States and other countries accepted GCD as a legitimate and valuable objective and agreed to give priority in disarmament negotiations to Khrushchev's proposal. Subsequently, both the United States and the Soviet Union tabled various formal proposals for GCD treaties.

Some analysts have supported general and complete disarmament as the only legitimate goal of disarmament negotiations. Those taking this approach, including at times the American and Soviet governments, have explicitly pointed to the desirability of limited arms-control measures as valuable steps on the road to GCD, since GCD could not be implemented in a single step. Limiting steps are also seen as valuable in providing experimentation with various forms of control and international organization to monitor disarmament agreements. Finally, such steps are seen as important in building international confidence, reducing tensions, and creating a political climate in which GCD could be negotiated and implemented.

Advocates of stabilized deterrence have argued either that GCD is unobtainable over the short run or, in fact, impossible to attain. They have contended that primary effort should be given to negotiating a treaty which would lead to the stabilization of the strategic forces of the United States and the Soviet Union at relatively low levels. Some advocates of this position proposed an agreement whereby each of the two superpowers would have a hundred missiles, perhaps on Polaris submarines cruising under the sea. This approach suggests that strategic forces should only be used to deter the strategic forces of the opponent and that other means should be found to deal with lesser threats. It implies also that if nuclear war does occur, each side would simply attack the cities of its opponent. It is because the notion of stabilized deterrence is tied to a particular strategy and seems to stress particular weapons systems that it has come under attack, not only from advocates of various flexible and controlled-response doctrines, but also from those who attempt to develop an approach to arms control which is independent of a specific strategy and a specific strategic situation.

An approach to arms control independent of strategy or strategic situation, the development of which lies behind much of the recent attention given to arms-control issues by strategic analysts, would focus on the objective to be pursued by military cooperation between potential enemies. Arms control, in this perspective, has three basic objectives: to reduce the likelihood of general nuclear war, particularly inadvertent general nuclear war; to reduce the damage expected if war occurs; and to reduce the cost of the arms race. Implicit also in this view is the need for general purpose local-war forces, as well as the strategic nuclear forces. Whether or not decreases in particular kinds of forces should be sought and whether a particular objective can be pursued more effectively by unilateral military action than by formal or tacit arms control are still open questions.

Adopting this last approach to arms control, we shall consider three issues of arms-control policy: first, whether or not the United States should continue to espouse the objective of general and complete disarmament; second, what can be done to combat the danger of the spread of nuclear weapons; and third, what arms-control measures may be possible in the area of strategic nuclear forces.

GENERAL AND COMPLETE DISARMAMENT

As was noted above, it is only since 1959 that the United States and the Soviet Union have explicitly committed themselves to seeking a treaty which would lead to general and complete disarmament. Is it sensible for the United States to continue to pursue this objective? Or alternatively, should the United States stress the need to seek more limited measures, not as a step towards GCD, but for their own sake in contributing to national and international security? Two questions may be asked about the policy of seeking GCD. First, is GCD a reasonable, practical objective? And second, even if it is not, is it sensible for the United States to espouse GCD?

All proposals for GCD permit nations to maintain forces necessary for internal security. How to calculate the forces necessary for this purpose is impossible to say; but it is clear that countries like South Vietnam, for example, might well be called upon to increase rather than decrease the size of their military establishment. And other countries, such as China, that use their military forces for a variety of internal purposes could presumably justify a force at current levels. In addition, the fact that Western proposals call for the creation of an international military force implies that the West is not, in effect, proposing GCD but rather the transfer of military force from under national control to international control.

Beyond this, we must ask whether there is, even in principle, such a thing as general and complete disarmament. We have already suggested that for political reasons—reasons for internal security—no state can accept the total elimination of military force. Beyond that, technology makes it impossible to rid oneself of military capability. The ability to make nuclear weapons cannot be forgotten nor even suppressed for any length of time in a society that relies on peaceful atomic energy, nor can the ability to deliver weapons be eliminated in any serious way in a society dedicated to intercontinental jet travel. Finally, man can never have taken from him all of the weapons which can be used for military purposes. Man can fight, although presumably with less immediate destruction, with his hands, his teeth, and with the primitive weapons that he will always have. Thus, on must compare the relative stability of various levels of weapons without pretending that there is some level which is zero or very close to zero.

It is also not certain that GCD, even if it were attainable in principle, would be a desirable objective for the United States to pursue. We are interested not in disarmament for its own sake but in peace in a just and secure world. It remains to be demonstrated that any of the values we have for the citizens of the United States or for citizens of other countries are more effectively pursued or obtained in a world without arms than in a world with moderate armaments under close control.

If GCD is, even in theory, an unreal state not necessarily in the interests of the United States, it remains to be asked: Why does the United States espouse this objective?

The initial stimulus that led to American support for GCD was, as has been noted, Soviet Premier Khrushchev's proposal for GCD. Faced with the Soviet proposal, the United States concluded that it had no alternative but to match it with a GCD plan of its own. It was believed, in the Eisenhower, Kennedy, and Johnson Administrations, that the United States would suffer a major propaganda defeat if it renounced GCD while the Soviets were continuing to favor it. It is thought that not only do the Soviets favor GCD but that nonaligned nations do also. In addition, there are some Americans, including some American policy makers, who believe that because very low levels of armament are clearly better than any higher levels, GCD is a practical and desirable goal.

Some advocates of GCD feel that the United States needs to embrace some utopia—needs to counteract the Communist ideology with a Western ideology based on the desire to turn swords into plowshares and to build a world of general and complete disarmament. However, even if one accepts the need for utopia, it is important to consider that GCD is not an end in itself, is not necessarily a part of utopia. The West can more effectively compete with the Soviet Union and Communist China if it stresses a utopia that includes freedom, justice, and an open society rather than elimination of arms for their own sake.

The commitment to GCD has led the United States to introduce proposals for treaties advocating general and complete disarmament in three stages. The drafting of these proposals and the subsequent changes that have been made in them has consumed much attention and time at arms-control conferences, at least through 1964. Confronting top leaders, including military leaders, with the scholastic problems of GCD treaties not only takes up time that might more fruitfully be spent in designing limited agreements but also gives to the whole process of developing arms-control proposals an unreal propaganda quality which undermines any belief in the utility and value of more limited steps as part of the search for national and international security. For this reason and because there may well be some significant limited steps that could be negotiated tacitly or formally with the Soviet Union, it might be useful for the United States simply to announce that in principle it is for GCD but that the negotiation of such an agreement at any time in the near future does not seem practical.

PREVENTING NUCLEAR PROLIFERATION

Since the dawn of the Nuclear Age, a number of observers have predicted that the spread of nuclear weapons to a large number of countries is inevitable and not necessarily undesirable. Others have pointed to the disastrous consequences that would result and have argued that the United States should take urgent steps to prevent the spread of nuclear weapons. The number of countries that have acquired nuclear weapons since the beginning of the Nuclear Age is probably smaller than almost anybody would have predicted in the late 1940's: only France and China joined the list of countries with advanced nuclear programs at the close of World War II; and even now only two other countries, India and Israel, appear to be close to making the decision to develop nuclear weapons.

There seems to be little doubt that the spread of nuclear weapons would not be in the interest of the United States. At one level it would simply reduce American influence and power in the world by increasing the number of countries capable of wreaking great destruction, if not on the United States, at least on other peoples. Moreover, all the countries that now have nuclear weapons are among the small groups of countries that have relatively stable internal political systems. The likelihood of internal dissident groups getting control of the weapons is small. Moreover, except for China, these countries are relatively well satisfied and do not have any irredentist claims. If nuclear weapons were to spread to less stable countries and regimes, the likelihood of nuclear weapons being used and, with it, the probability of a general nuclear war would undoubtedly increase greatly. Local nuclear wars are more apt to break out between countries such as India and Pakistan, or India and China, or the Arab states and Israel. Countries that have resorted to violence against each other in the postwar period—countries that feel their very existence may be at stake in any war—may find compelling reasons to use nuclear weapons, while the major nuclear powers, which have not engaged in conflicts threatening their own existence, do not see any reason to use these weapons. The increased probability that nuclear weapons would be used in local conflicts would make our world a much less pleasant and more dangerous place in which to live—a world in which American policy makers would have to devote much more attention than they now do to containing or preventing local conflict and a world in which any crisis could lead to the introduction of nuclear weapons by a number of different states or perhaps a number of different groups.

For all these reasons, the United States is—at least publicly—committed to trying to halt the spread of nuclear weapons. There appears to be no possibility, at least in the short run, of reducing the number of nuclear powers from five; although, over the long run, Britain and France may both be willing to merge their nuclear capabilities into a European nuclear force.

With the dawn of the Nuclear Age, atomic weapons were described as the great equalizer that would make it possible for any country to develop a force on a par in power with that of any other. The growing cost and complexity of delivery systems and the ability to destroy enemy delivery systems before they can be used make it clear that the superpowers will continue to dominate over any other powers. It remains true, however, that nuclear weapons substantially increase the military capability of a state and at a much smaller cost than the development of conventional systems. The cost of producing nuclear weapons and delivery systems and the technical problems involved have perceptibly decreased and will continue to do so. Thus, in trying to prevent the spread of nuclear weapons, we must work essentially on the incentives of various states rather than directly on their capabilities.

The extent to which formal arms-control measures can—and must—play a role in preventing the spread of nuclear weapons remains an open question. Basically, the solution is to increase the political cost to various countries of proceeding with a nuclear program. This can be done by increasing the technological cost of nuclear programs, by trying to restrict technological information, by threatening various kinds of economic and political sanctions against countries that proceed with nuclear programs, and by attempting to enhance the belief that nuclear weapons will not be used in any conflict. In order for the United States to implement a program pursuing these objectives, it would have to pay certain costs: first, whatever cost is involved in attempting to bring pressure to bear on proud and independent governments; secondly, the price of somewhat reducing American willingness to use nuclear weapons, since the United States would be arguing that such weapons cannot—and will not—be used. When and if the United States is prepared to pay these political costs, it would need to outline a program dealing generally with the problem of nuclear proliferation and specifically with the threats imposed by India's and Israel's efforts to become nuclear powers.

A major motivation for the nuclear test ban treaty was the belief that it would help to prevent the spread of nuclear weapons. In 1965 both the United States and the Soviet Union tabled, for the first time, formal treaties designed to deal specifically with the threat of the proliferation of nuclear weapons. Both treaties called upon the nuclear powers to agree not to transfer nuclear weapons or information about the testing of nuclear weapons to other countries. The treaties also provided for an agreement among the non-nuclear nations not to make nuclear weapons nor to accept them from nuclear powers. The draft proposed by the

United States, however, permitted the transfer of nuclear weapons to an alliance nuclear force, such as the proposed NATO multi-lateral force, while the Soviet draft not only prevented such transfers but in fact called for the removal of nuclear weapons from the territory of all non-nuclear powers. The differences between the two drafts reflected, in part, a greater Soviet preoccupation with the danger of nuclear proliferation in Europe, specifically in Germany, and American preoccupation with the more general problem of proliferation in countries of the third world. More-over, it probably reflected the desire of both countries to gain political advantage from any proliferation treaty, by solidifying or breaking up NATO, and to force their opponents to pay a greater part of the cost involved in trying to prevent the spread of nuclear weapons.

The proliferation problem provides a good instance of an issue that appears on the surface to be basically an arms-control issue but that turns out in fact to be a political issue. It could be dealt with by arms-control agreements but could be handled in other ways also, if the superpowers were willing to deal with it.

THE STRATEGIC ARMS RACE

The attention given to propaganda and negotiations for forces that might be used in a general nuclear war has been focused on the effort to draft a treaty for general and complete disarmament and, more recently, on the American proposal for a freeze on the numbers and characteristics of strategic delivery systems. How-ever, in practice, the emphasis has been on unilateral moves and tacit negotiations. The implementation by the United States of a strategy of controlled response, with its better command and con-trol over strategic forces; the possibility of using strategic forces in limited ways; and the desire to be in a position to negotiate the end of a general nuclear war—all reflect concentration on the common interests between the United States and the Soviet Un-ion, namely, preventing accidental war and reducing the expected damage should war occur.

There has also been a major effort to reduce the cost and risks of the strategic arms race. By risks we mean not only the threat that the forces might be used in a nuclear war but also the effect on the political environment posed by a reduction in economic costs. The strategic budget of the United States fell very rapidly from 1962 to 1965; the United States did not increase its planned procurement of strategic offensive forces and had, at least until mid-1966, refrained from the production of ballistic-missile defenses. This restraint in procurement has resulted in a kind of interaction between the United States and the Soviet Union. The questions come to mind: What would be a likely Soviet response, for example, to an American procurement of ballistic-missile defense? Can the Soviets nullify the effectiveness of the defense by much lower expenditures on offensive weapons?

Thus, perhaps the most important arms-control agreement between the United States and the Soviet Union in the early 1960's has been the restraint shown on both sides—though perhaps more on the American than the Soviet—in the procurement of strategic offensive and defensive systems. This is an agreement that would have been almost impossible to write or formalize in any way but that nevertheless served as an important break in the strategic arms race. This restraint, coupled with an emphasis on both sides on well-protected, well-controlled systems, has gone very far towards reducing the danger of either inadvertent or deliberate general war, increasing the possibilities for reducing damage if war occurred, and reducing the cost of the arms race and its political impact. This is not to say that formal arms-control measures would not have also contributed to these objectives, but rather that tacit understandings and informal arrangements may accomplish many of the objectives pursued through arms control.

SELECTED BIBLIOGRAPHY

Brennan, Donald G., ed. *Arms Control, Disarmament and National Security.* New York: George Braziller, 1961.

Bull, Hedley. *The Control of the Arms Race.* New York: Frederick A Praeger, 1965.

Levine, Robert A. *The Arms Debate.* Cambridge, Mass.: Harvard University Press, 1963.

Schelling, Thomas C., and Morton H. Halperin. *Strategy and Arms Control.* New York: Twentieth Century Fund, 1961.

Stone, Jeremy J. *Containing the Arms Race.* Cambridge, Mass.: M.I.T University Press, 1966.

Index